LIVING FREE

By

James F. Sunnock

Living Free

Table of Contents

You can be saved, but still be messed up.

Chapter 1

Redeeming the Entire Person

"Now the Lord is spirit, and where the Spirit of Lord is, there is freedom" (2 Corinthians 3:17 NIV).

I am excited that you picked up this book to begin what I hope will be a life changing experience. "Living Free" begins with a desire to be free. Free from past disappointments, hurts, strongholds and addictions. Throughout the pages to follow you will realize that freedom is actually a journey and way of life.

The origins of this book began fifteen years ago. It has been an amazing journey and by chronicling life's discoveries, I want to offer hope to those who have given up, renew the dream for the ones that feel destiny has eluded them, and assure all that Jesus Christ has come to proclaim directly to you the Good News that He truly does heal the broken heart and still sets the captives free as He promised in Luke 4:18. He has provided you and I with an abundant life! The only catch, it will cost you everything, but it is so worth it!

For me this journey of Living Free began in the summer of 2001 as I sat down by a lake early in the morning. A friend could see that my life, as well as my wife's, was on empty and he allowed us to spend some time at his cabin in solitude to be able to hopefully rest, reflect and recharge. In the previous two months we had moved with our three boys, ages 12, 10 and 9, to pastor a small church in Battle Creek, Michigan, tried to sell our house on our own, suffered the loss of my wife's brother to suicide, only to be back in the funeral home ten days later to mourn the passing of her father, all while trying to bring a new vision and direction to a small failing church. There was nothing left in the tank and now I found myself staring at a lake in Northern Michigan. I'm not even sure how long I had been staring and just thinking, "Lord, if your Word is true, and we are what your Word says we are, then why don't I see more victory in my life and the lives of other believers? Why is there divorce and brokenness in the church? Why do I feel that for every step forward I take, I seem to slip back two?" Then Luke 4:18 was spoken to my heart, *"The Spirit of the LORD is upon Me, Because He has anointed Me To preach the gospel to the poor; He has sent Me to heal the brokenhearted, to proclaim liberty to the captives and recovery of sight to the blind, to set at liberty those who are oppressed."* I knew then that my heavenly Father was calling me on a journey. Not just a personal journey for me alone, but a journey that would enable me to show others how freedom is for all who seek Him with a sincere heart in the context of the powerful and eternal principles of the Kingdom of God.

As we embark on this subject of freedom, let me begin by asking you a few important questions: How do you define freedom? What does a free person feel like and act like? What does freedom look like? How do you achieve real freedom? Please take a few minutes to really think about that before continuing to read. Then, after you have seriously

6

contemplated those questions, put your answer in writing. You may want to even jot your response in the margin of this page or possibly you will want to enter it into a journal that you keep. But I encourage you to record it somewhere so you can refer back to your answer later.

In order to fully understand the subject of true freedom, as well as the reason for the overt and covert bondages we may experience, we must have an understanding of how God created us. Because, you will see that God will redeem us in relationship to how He created us.

It is vitally important to understanding that God has created us with a spirit, a soul and a body. Since He has created us in this manner, He also has a distinct and separate redemptive plan for each of those areas of our life. Let's define each of these areas:

Spirit – Our spirit is the eternal part of our being.

Soul – Our soul is made up of our mind, will and emotions.

Body – Our body is the mortal and temporal part of our being.

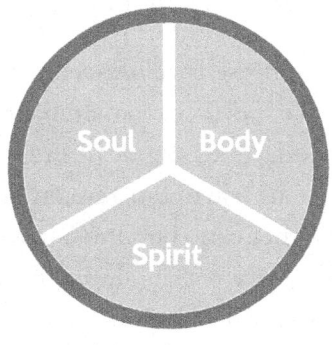

Redeeming Our Body

As I mentioned previously, God has a plan of redemption for each one of these three elements that make up who He has created us to be.

Let's first consider the redemption of the body. The redemption of the BODY is in the **future.** The Bible tells us that the body will be redeemed in the future at the time of the resurrection at Christ's return. In fact, we are promised a new body when Jesus returns. That is, our body will be "saved" (redeemed or glorified) at this specific time designated in the future. We don't know exactly when that will be, but we do know the Scriptures declare it to be a certain reality at some time in the future. Here is what the Bible says:

> "Behold, I tell you a mystery: We shall not all sleep, but we shall all be changed – in a moment, in the twinkling of an eye, at the last trumpet. For the trumpet will sound, and the dead will be raised incorruptible, and we shall be changed. For this corruptible must put on incorruption and this mortal must put on immortality" (1 Corinthians 15:51-53 NKJV).

> "For the Lord Himself will descend from heaven with a shout, with the voice of an archangel, and with the trumpet of God. And the dead in Christ will rise first. Then we who are alive and remain shall be caught up together with them in the clouds to meet the Lord in the air. And thus we shall always be with the Lord" (I Thessalonians 4:16-17 NKJV).

Redeeming Our Spirit

Next, let's talk about the redemption of our spirit. Our spirit is saved or redeemed the very moment we accept Jesus Christ to become the Lord and Savior of our lives. So, the redemption of the SPIRIT is **instant**. Notice what Ephesians 2:8 says about the redemption of our spirit:

> "For by grace you have been saved through faith, and that not of yourselves; it is the gift of God" (NKJV).

Notice the tense of the verb in this passage is in the past tense. That means it has already been completed. You "have been" saved through faith. It isn't something that is ongoing; rather, it is an action that took place the very second you asked Jesus to come into your life.

Your spirit is eternal and lasts for all of eternity – it never dies. It is the choice you make while you are alive that determines if you have eternal life (heaven) or eternal death (hell). Everyone has eternity in their future, but God has given us the ability to choose where we desire to spend eternity.

It is very important to understand that the spirit has a process of redemption that is distinct and separate from the soul and the body. When we accept Christ as our personal savior, our spirit is made new instantaneously. Romans 10:9-10 says, "...if you confess with your mouth the Lord Jesus and believe in your heart that God has raised Him from the dead, you will be saved. [10] For with the heart one believes unto righteousness, and with the mouth confession is made unto salvation" (NKJV).

In the very instant you confess with your mouth and believe in your heart, in that very moment, your spirit is made new and transformed; you are immediately "born again." 2 Corinthians 5:7 confirms this: "Therefore, if anyone is in Christ, he is a new creation; the **old has gone**, the new has come" (NIV). It happens instantly! As soon as we declare Jesus as Lord of our life, our spirit is instantly and forever changed and redeemed. It's not the same old spirit, but a new creation which enables our name to be written in heaven; the old spirit is gone and the new spirit is alive in Christ.

Here is where many Christians get tripped up. Either by past teaching, personal study, or simply by assumption, some people think that when the spirit is made new, that is, when they accept Jesus into their life, every aspect of their life should be made new. This leads to confusion and often discouragement as people try to live a Christian life.

There is often confusion between the redemption of the spirit and the redemption of the soul. When you don't understand the difference between spirit and soul, it's easy to question your salvation. This can also lead to working or striving for salvation, which then leads to discouragement and feeling as though we failed at being saved. The reality is that when your spirit is redeemed and transformed, your soul (mind, will and emotions) still has to go through the process of redemption.

I remember exactly where I was the day I asked Jesus into my life. However, the next morning when I woke up I realized I was still stuck in the same way of thinking. I was stuck with the hurts, wounds and baggage of my past. I was frustrated because I thought it was going to be a game changer, but it wasn't a game changer in the way I thought it would be. It was a game changer on an eternal and spiritual level, but when it came to my mind, I still struggled with the things I struggled with before I accepted Jesus. I still carried the same stress, anxieties and worries. Why? Because, my soul (my mind, will and emotions), still needed to be renewed. In other words, I needed to "work out" (not "work for") my salvation in my soul. Philippians 2:12 encourages us in this way, "Therefore, my beloved, as you have always obeyed, not as in my presence only, but now much more in my absence, work out your own salvation with fear and trembling" (NKJV).

It's very important to understand that it is the blood of Jesus that saves us…period. It's not the blood of Jesus plus some other behavior like reading the Bible, praying or going to church. It is simply and solely accepting the blood of Jesus that saves our spirit. There are no "good works" we can do to obtain God's grace to redeem our spirit. Please hear this very clearly: You cannot redeem your spirit by doing the "right" things. The redemption of your spirit is purely an act of grace that comes as a result of our acceptance of the gift of God's only begotten son, Jesus. Ephesians 2:8-9 makes this very clear: "For it is by grace you have been saved, through faith – and this is not from yourselves, it is the gift of God – not by works, so that no one can boast" (Ephesians 2:8-9 NIV).

So, here is the bottom line. You can be saved but still be "messed up." The purpose of my writing is to let people know that just because you make mistakes, experience anxiety, have a temper or have difficulty overcoming a myriad of problems in your life does not mean you're not saved. Your spirit has been saved because Jesus died on the cross for you and you accepted His sacrifice as atonement for your sins. Rejoice and be thankful for the redemption of your spirit with which God has blessed you!

First things first

Jesus begins His ministry by reading out of the scroll of Isaiah

> Luke 4:18 *"The Spirit of the* LORD *is upon Me,* Because He has anointed Me *To preach the gospel to the* poor; He has sent Me to heal the brokenhearted, To proclaim liberty to the *captives* And recovery of sight to the *blind,* To *set at liberty those who are* oppressed; (NKJV)

Two things we can draw upon this proclamation is: One, only Jesus can heal the broken heart and set captives free and second, You have to heal the spirit before you can heal the heart.

There's one question every person has to reconcile… Is my life right with God? Some will say, "I try to be a good person and do the right thing." Trying harder to be good, doesn't make you connected or right with God. The bible says in

> Romans 10:13 For *"whoever calls* on the name of the LORD shall be saved." That means it's not enough to just believe there is a God or to try harder to be good, but there has to be a moment where one realized that without Christ in my life and can't make it in this life or in eternity. It's a moment where you call out to Jesus to be rescued and surrender your life. I remember exactly where I was when that moment came to me. If you

don't have a defining moment, this is your moment. Salvation in Christ is something that no one is good enough to earn. It's a gift He offers to those who ask for it, or call on His name and surrender. (NKJV)

Ephesians 2:8–9 For by grace you have been saved through faith, and that not of yourselves; *it is* the gift of God, [9] not of works, lest anyone should boast. (NKJV)

No one can brag, because none of us deserves it. If you haven't done so already, let Jesus heal, transform and rescue you spirit, so that He can begin healing and setting free your soul.

It's simple but not easy. It's simple because all it takes is a simple prayer from your heart. It's not easy, because it requires we let go of control and completely surrender our trust and life to Him.

Romans 10:9 "That is you confess with your mouth the Lord Jesus and believe in your heart that God has raised him from the dead, you will be saved." (NKJV)

Redeeming Our Soul

Please pay very close attention to the information I am about to share with you. It can be life changing for you! The redemption and transformation of the soul is the epicenter of this entire book and it is crucial to comprehend this concept if you want to experience freedom and abundant living in this lifetime.

The redemption of the soul (mind, will, and emotions) is ongoing. Even though our spirit is saved at this point, our soul still needs to be transformed, changed and renewed. That's why I said earlier that you can be saved, but still be "messed up." So, the natural question then is, "How do we work out the salvation of the soul?"

It is important to understand that while we are in the process of figuring this out, we are still promised Heaven because our spirit is saved. And, unlike needing to wait for the coming of Christ to experience the redemption of our body, we can begin now to experience changes in our mind, will and emotions. I don't think any of us want to wait until we die to experience all the healing and transformation that is in store for us. But, again, the big question is, "How do we renew or transform our mind?"

We can experience the transformation of our soul (mind, will and emotions) while we live our lives here on earth; the same miracle transformation that happened to our spirit when we accepted Christ can also happen to our soul when we become His disciples and commit to renewing our mind by God's Word. In fact, if we are sincerely seeking after God and His will for our lives, we should expect transformation.

> John 8:31-32: "To the Jews who had believed him, Jesus said, 'If you hold to my teaching, you are really my disciples. Then you will know the truth, and the truth will set you free'" (NIV).

God's Word doesn't just give us knowledge and insight, but it supernaturally transforms our soul. Romans 12:2 confirms this and instructs us in this way, "Do not conform any longer to the pattern of this world, but be transformed by the renewing of your mind. Then you will be able to test and approve what God's will is – his good, pleasing and perfect will" (NIV).

Unfortunately, this is how many Christians read this passage: "We should read our Bible so we better understand how we should behave and live." But, that's not what it says! God doesn't tell us how to live; rather, He transforms our mind, giving us the ability and desire to live a Godly, abundant life.

According to 2 Corinthians 10:5 God has given us the ability to "…demolish arguments and every pretension that sets itself up against the knowledge of God, and we take **captive** every thought to make it obedient to Christ" (NIV). That's right, you have the ability to "demolish arguments" and "take captive" every thought to make it obedient to Christ. This is a very powerful promise!

Let's unpack this verse further. The Greek word for "captive" is "aichmalotizontes," which is derived from the root words "aichme" (spear) and "halosis" (capture). It is a military term meaning to take complete control and describes when an enemy was taken captive and they would tie their hands and poke them in the back with a spear and force them to march down the street to be displayed as conquered.

God's Word is a sword and is used to take every thought captive: "Take…the sword of the Spirit, which is the word of God" –Ephesians 6:17 NIV. The Bible isn't a bunch of instructions about what to do, but it supernaturally transforms us, giving us the power to change our thoughts and actions as

15

we live out our relationship with God, enabling us to do the will of God. It changes us from the inside out; whereas, we have a tendency to try to focus on changing just our behavior without experiencing a transformation of our mind, will and emotions.

Jesus said, "I am the vine; you are the branches. If you remain in me and I in you, you will bear much fruit; apart from me you can do nothing" (John 15:5 NIV).

By using the Sword of the Spirit (as we read in Ephesians 6:17 above) and by abiding in Christ (John 15:5), we then have a different perspective. With this perspective and empowerment, "We demolish arguments and every pretension that sets itself up against the knowledge of God, and we take captive every thought to make it obedient to Christ" (2 Corinthians 10:5 NIV). And then we will "bear much fruit" (John 15:5a NIV). Let's face it; apart from Jesus we will never be able to live the abundant life God has promised us in His Word. Our ongoing faith relationship with Jesus is the catalyst for taking captive every thought that will try to destroy us.

This tells us that we are to strive toward renewing and transforming our mind, will and emotions. We cannot remain stagnant when it comes to this part of our life. This is what Jesus was referring to in John 10:10 when he promised us the abundant life: "The thief does not come except to steal, and to kill and to destroy. I have come that they may have life, and that they may have it more abundantly" (NKJV).

You see, trying harder is not the answer. Unfortunately, as believers we think now that we're saved, it's up to us to try harder to be a good person. We think that being a Christian is a set of standards by which we should now live. We think, "I just need to try harder now that I have Jesus in my life." But, again, trying harder is not the answer.

Allow me to share a modern day parable of sorts. I would say, "The Kingdom of God is like starting a lawn mower." When I was a boy I was the kid in the neighborhood that mowed everyone's lawns. My dad taught me to clean the mower once a week as proper maintenance. It was his mower, but he let me use it and I paid him a little bit of money from my earnings from each lawn I mowed for the use of the mower.

One day I hopped on my bike. Grabbing the lawn mower handle with one hand and steering my bike with the other hand, I peddled to one of the neighbors' houses, with lawn mower in tow, to mow their lawn. After parking my bike and getting the lawn mower in place on the lawn, I went through the proper starting procedure my father expertly taught me. I pushed the little rubber button a couple of times to prime the engine as instructed. Then I pulled and pulled and pulled on the starting cord, but I just could not get the mower to start.

After multiple pulling attempts, I was beginning to get frustrated and after several tries, I took it to a new level of intensity. I primed it some more, then pulled and pulled and pulled. I repeated the process a few times. When I started smelling gas I knew I flooded the mower. So I paced back and forth with nervous energy as I let the mower set until I could try to start it again. After several minutes I primed it again and kept pulling the starter cord, over and over again.

I distinctly remember becoming so enraged and angry at that stupid lawn mower that I tried longer and harder pulls. When that didn't work I tried short, fast pulls. When that didn't work I resorted to yelling at the lawn mower and telling it how stupid it was. Finally, I stepped back and did the manly thing; I kicked it out of pure frustration and anger. When I kicked it I broke a pulley to the self-propelling mechanism. At that point I knew I was a dead man because my father was likely going to kill me. Things went from bad to worse. Not only would the lawn mower not start, now I was mad at myself for breaking the pulley. I remember literally throwing a temper tantrum in my neighbor's yard.

The neighbor saw my plight and my unfortunate reaction and came up to me and asked, "Can I help?" Out of pure frustration and probably some embarrassment I reluctantly agreed to receive his assistance. He looked at the mower, bent down, and connected the spark plug wire to the spark plug. My dad always taught me to disconnect the spark plug before cleaning the blades so the blade couldn't engage and hurt me. Evidently, I didn't reconnect it after the last cleaning. After the spark plug wire was connected, the mower started on the first pull.

Many people have lived their Christian life much like that; thinking if they just pulled harder, this thing would work. If they prime it enough, it has to work. But, trying harder in our own strength can often lead to greater frustration and make things worse and even cause greater damage.

You see, Jesus may be in a person's heart, but they may still struggle with depression, anger, addictions or some other issue.

And, they think it's all because they aren't pulling or priming hard enough or getting the sequence right. Many of us live with a false theology that says if we will just pull harder or work harder, things will get better. But the reality is that nothing will change until we plug into the power source.

The spirit needs to be healed before the heart can be healed.

Chapter 2

God has a Plan to Renew Your Soul

We have already established the fact that if we have accepted Christ as our personal Lord and Savior, our body will be redeemed in the future and our spirit was transformed immediately. But, just how do we renew our soul (mind, will and emotions)? How do we heal our hurts and emotional pain? How do we get to the place where our soul is truly transformed, completely healed and set free? Thankfully, the Word of God is very clear when it comes to this matter.

In the fourth chapter of Luke we find Jesus talking to people that were "trying to get their lawn mowers started" just by pulling harder. Not literally, of course. But they were stuck; trapped by the brutality of life. The people Jesus ministered to while he was on earth ranged from those who were steeped in religious laws and traditions to those considered to be the outcasts of their society and the lowest of the low. Jesus knew exactly what needs existed in these people and he also knew the answer.

Recognizing their pain, this is what He said: "The Spirit of the Lord is upon Me, because He has anointed Me to preach the gospel to the poor; He has sent Me to heal the brokenhearted, to proclaim liberty to the captives and recovery of sight to the blind, to set at liberty those who are oppressed" (Luke 4:18-19 NKJV).

The devil seemed to be well aware of the potential impact Jesus would have over the course of his ministry because he did everything within his power to put an abrupt halt to the Son of God who was to take away the sin of mankind and return humanity back to its right relationship with our Heavenly Father. Before Jesus spoke the words referenced above, he was baptized, the Spirit descended upon Him, and then He spent 40 days in the wilderness where He was tempted by the devil. The devil made many attempts to stop the ministry of Jesus from going forward and to stop Him from uttering the words in Luke 4:18-19 which would establish for all eternity to destiny for which Jesus was placed on this earth as incarnate man.

But the attempts of the devil were futile when it came to thwarting the plan of the Almighty God. It was the devil's plan to keep mankind broken, lost and without hope. But in the midst of the all encompassing chaos brought upon by the sin of Adam and Eve in the Garden, Jesus, with the utterance of his Luke 4 proclamation, established the plan whereby he would heal the brokenhearted, set captives free and set at liberty those who were oppressed!

It is vitally important to understand that there is no healing apart from Christ. In order to heal your soul (mind, will and emotions), your spirit must first be healed. The redemption of your spirit is the foundation for the healing of your soul. While counselors, doctors and medication can contribute or assist in helping us cope with anxiety and emotional brokenness, **only Jesus can heal your heart, soul, mind, will and emotions.**

We have all seen cars driving around with one of those small temporary spare tires called a "donut". Chances are you've seen cars driving around on one of those and you can tell it's been on there for awhile and that they have no intention of replacing it anytime soon. Medication is like putting one of those small temporary "donut tires" on your car. There are times you really need one of those tires in life. You may need something to help you through a very difficult time. No one has the right to tell you that you can't use counselors or medication because we know they do serve a valuable purpose. However, that is not the permanent solution. Please understand that there is no shame in using medication when needed. In fact, I encourage you to get good Christian counseling. But also understand, Christ alone is the permanent solution because He alone can bring healing and freedom.

During our journey, when we don't look to Christ as the answer, we often seek relief from emotional pain and baggage through behavioral changes or self-control. In the course of my ministry I have observed there are four traps people fall into when trying to "fix" themselves.

Trap #1 - The Inner Vow

Often people will make inner vows as a means to protect themselves, thinking this will be the catalyst to their change. These individuals will say things like, "I will never let anyone close enough to hurt me like that again" or "I will never forgive that person" or "From now on I will just take care of it myself." When we make inner vows, we choose to become the "god" over that area of our life. We take that authority from God and we become lord over that area.

There is an individual in the church I pastor who always carried a silver dollar in his pocket. There was a distinct time in his life when he made an inner vow, "I will never be broke and to make sure of that I will always carry this silver dollar to remind me." It was a vow that *he* made; instead of trusting God, *he* was going to take care of it *himself.* His inner vow was based on a past hurt and the resulting lie he believed. Of course, that silver dollar couldn't even buy a gallon of gasoline today. But, it was symbolic of the vow he made years ago that was based on the pain he experienced in his life.

During a time of prayer in the midst of a church building program, he asked, "Lord, what is my part to be in expanding the Kingdom of God?" Guess what the first thing was that God asked him to give? That's right, the silver dollar. You see, God didn't want his money, he wanted his heart. He was obedient to God and put the silver dollar in the offering the following Sunday and also gave a generous gift.

He told me later, "Giving the big financial gift was easy, but it nearly killed me to reach inside my pocket and drop into the offering basket that silver dollar. But, as soon as I did, I was healed and set free."

Trap #2 - We Seek Relief in Our Own Ways

Seeking relief in your own way will always lead to bondage and greater frustration. Some will turn to addictions to try to find an escape or relief from their situation. Some will cling to certain false beliefs about themselves or their circumstances. Some will simply stagnate and cease to progress in their Christian walk. These scenarios are played out in many ways, but none of them will bring a person to the place of healing and wholeness they desire. By trying to fix the problem ourselves, we are actually exacerbating the disconnection our soul (mind, will and emotions) has with God which is the real issue. We must realize that only by turning to our Heavenly Father will we find truth and healing.

Trap #3 – Emotional Blindness

There is an emotional blindness that many believers experience that causes them to have faith that Jesus can redeem their spirit, but He can't heal their mind and emotions. The way we see things can indeed keep our soul from being healed. 2 Corinthians 3:15-16 says, "Even to this day when Moses (Old Testament Law) is read, a veil covers their hearts. But whenever anyone turns to the Lord, the veil is taken away" (NIV). Sometimes Christians have a "veil of blindness" that covers their spiritual eyes causing them to believe that God is not big enough to heal their emotional pain and the unforgiveness that may plague them. Or, they go into a state of denial, ignoring the issue and just keep "pushing through life." But they never truly experience freedom.

Instead, they get caught in a system of trying harder. They lose hope and sink into the belief that this is just the way life is going to be for them; a life of misery and defeat.

Trap #4 - We Become "Functional" and Believe We Don't Need Healing

We become so ingrained in our hurt that it becomes our identity. So much that we don't even know what a healed/free life would be like. After dealing with our issues for long enough, we can easily fall into a position of complacency. That is, we become "functional" in how we have dealt with our past and then believe we don't need healing. We're driving around with a spare donut tire. Our proverbial car is going down the road, so why bother getting our tire fixed?

In our mind, it becomes easier to push down the lid on our emotions and plow through life rather than face the pain and handing it over to our Heavenly Father. That is, People lose hope. Many people succumb to the false belief that "It's too late for me." They contend, "It's impossible to change" and they simply give up hope. Proverbs 13:12 so aptly defines this scenario: "Hope deferred makes the heart sick, but *when* the desire comes, *it is* a tree of life" (NKJV).

YOU NEED TO KNOW THERE IS HOPE! Here are some of God's reassuring truths:

John 8:32 (NKJV): "And you shall know the truth, and the truth shall make you free."

Psalm 34:18 (NIV): "The Lord is close to the brokenhearted and saves those who are crushed in spirit" (NIV).

1John 4:4 (KJV): "...greater is He that is in you than he that is in the world."

Galatians 2:20 (NIV): "I have been crucified with Christ and **I no longer live, but Christ lives in me**. The life I live in the body, I live by faith in the Son of God, who loved me and gave himself for me."

26

I encourage you to re-read these scriptural promises above. Then, ask Father to give you revelation and speak to your heart about how they personally apply to you and what they mean for your life.

Notice in Galatians 2:20 above that this verse doesn't tell us we need to try harder; rather it reveals to us that His power lives through us, allowing us to live in the victory for which He died. In this passage the Apostle Paul is basically telling us that the life of the believer is no longer the life of the believer. Instead, the life of the believer comes from the One in whom we believe.

Often the enemy of our soul can read our Bible to us. He may tell us Jesus died for us so we should try harder to do better so it will look to everyone else that we are acting just like Jesus. Many people are trying very hard, but don't have the spark plug connected – they aren't fully connected to the power source.

In other words, many believe being a Christian means to "just try harder to be like Jesus"….to pull harder and harder. But that is very far from the truth. No matter how hard you try, you will never be able to figure out how to heal your soul (mind, will and emotions). That is something only God can do. You see, God desires to heal your broken heart and renew your heart just as He was able to redeem your spirit.

When people ask me questions about the reasons specific things have happened in their life or what they should be doing, I will often give them this very simple, yet very powerful, answer, "I don't know, let's ask Father." I offer this response because I know God is the only one that can answer their question and I want them to understand that God desires to communicate with them on a very personal and intimate basis. God has a definite plan to renew your soul.

There is HOPE – you can be healed and set free! Blood saves, water sets free.

It is important to understand that sitting on the branch of "good" is not good, because you are sitting in the wrong tree.

Chapter 3

Connecting to the Power Source: The Story of Two Trees

Let's talk about what it means or looks like to be connected to the power source. To understand the power source to which God desires us to be connected we have to go back to the Garden of Eden where mankind's relationship with God was originally established. It is from this beginning that we discover the reality of what it means to be "connected" to the divine life source which will ultimately bring healing to the brokenhearted, sight to the blind, and liberty to the captive.

The Story of Two Trees

"Now the Lord God had planted a garden in the east, in Eden; and there He put the man He had formed. And the Lord God made all kinds of trees grow out of the ground – trees that were pleasing to the eye and good for food. In the middle of the garden were the tree of life AND the tree of the knowledge of good and evil" (Genesis 2:8-9 NIV).

There are only two trees referenced in Genesis 2:8-9: The Tree of Life and The Tree of the Knowledge of Good and Evil.

Notice that the knowledge of good is part of the tree that also contains the knowledge of evil.

Before the fall, Adam and Eve received life sustaining sustenance from the Tree of Life. It was while they ate from this tree that they enjoyed communion and fellowship with God. God communicated directly with them and there was peace and harmony in their existence. There was absolutely no indication of even a hint of discord, conflict or separation regarding that relationship.

However, it was very clear that they were forbidden to eat the fruit from the Tree of the Knowledge of Good and Evil. Yet, Adam and Eve thought the fruit on this tree looked very desirable and the serpent convinced them no harm would come to them if they ate of the tree. So, they ate from the forbidden tree and, as a result, altered their relationship with the eternal God who then banished them from the garden. And thus began the struggle of mankind to live in right relationship with God.

So, how does that relate to each of us living in today's world? We have already established that if we have confessed our sins, asked for forgiveness and accepted Jesus as our Lord and Savior, our spirit has already been redeemed. That is, our spirit abides in the Tree of Life. At the very moment we made our confession of faith in Christ our spirit was restored to right relationship with God and we again became able to partake of the Tree of Life and abide there. However, our soul (mind, will and emotions) still resides in the Tree of the Knowledge of Good and Evil.

So, the million dollar question is, "How do we get our soul (mind, will and emotions) out of the Tree of the Knowledge of Good and Evil and into the Tree of Life where our spirit resides?" The answer to that question is the exact purpose of this book; to help you now connect your soul to the Tree of Life so you can live the abundant life God desires for you.

The Bible refers to this as renewing our mind upon the word of God. It's not about learning more about God and trying harder, but being with Him and enjoying the same fellowship that Adam and Eve experienced in the Garden of Eden.

The reason many don't see victory in their life is because they rely on their own strength. Their soul is still in the Tree of Knowledge, but simply moved from a branch of "evil" to a branch of "good which isn't really good at all because it's in the wrong tree. We simply develop a life where we have some good days and some bad days.

We even have a tendency to build tree houses in this tree with the intention of taking up permanent residency. There is a television program I enjoy watching about an individual who has made a business out of building extremely elaborate and often exotic tree houses for his clients. We often do the same thing on a spiritual level. We build tree houses in the Tree of the Knowledge of Good and Evil where things are familiar and it keeps us in the very tree in which we were never meant to live. However, by staying there we will never know or experience the fullness of the abundant life God has promised us.

We need to move to the Tree of Life and encounter true transformation, healing and victory. God doesn't want you to live by "coping with things" or "just getting by."

Dr. Bob Hamp refers to this way of life with his own parable. He suggests a person's life in the Tree of the Knowledge of Good and Evil is like a "dirty diaper." Here is what he means: We come to God with our sin, He cleans us up, and we are given a "clean diaper." That is, he takes away our sin and gives us the opportunity to live for Him in such a way that would be pleasing to Him. We then go along in life, we mess up and now we have a "dirty diaper" again. We take our mess to God, we repent, He cleans us up and gives us a clean diaper once again. We try harder for a period of time only to once again mess up something in our lives giving us another "dirty diaper."

We soon begin to think that a life in Christ is merely taking our messes to God, allowing Him to clean us up, and then we go on until we need to be changed again. Although God is willing to take our messes and clean us up, our life in Him is meant to be so much more.

If you ever have had young children, you know that something happens around the age of 3 to 4 years old. Suddenly they come to a place of maturity and "transformation" where they no longer need a diaper because they now know how to have certain controls over their own body. A very similar thing happens to us as we mature in Christ. We come to a place where we understand we don't have to "mess up" any longer. That is, we don't have to do the things we were accustomed to doing that would inevitably cause us to sin and interfere with our relationship with God.

34

God can do more than just take your messes and send you back to try harder. When you connect to Him (The Tree of LIFE), He will transform you, heal you and set you free.

It's important to understand that sitting on the branch of "good" is not good at all because you're sitting in the wrong tree. The Tree of Knowledge tells us to prime and pull; prime and pull. You may remember from the lawn mower illustration I shared earlier, I pulled and pulled on that starter cord until I was exhausted. But how hard did I have to pull when the spark plug wire was connected to the power source? It started on the first pull!

In the Garden of Eden, as long as Adam and Eve ate from the Tree of Life they were connected with God, fellowshipped with Him and knew Him. The Bible even says God walked with them. However, when Adam and Eve ate from the Tree of the Knowledge of Good and Evil, they unplugged from the Tree of Life (they disconnected the spark plug) and set the stage for all mankind.

At that point, a plan had to be set to get us plugged back into the Tree of Life. That's exactly what Jesus did on the cross - He died so we could come back to this Tree of Life. When we confessed Jesus as our Lord and Savior, our spirit was immediately reconnected to the Tree of Life. In John 15:5 (NIV) Jesus invites us to "abide in Him" so we can bear much fruit: "I am the vine; you are the branches. If a man remains in me and I in him, he will bear much fruit; apart from me you can do nothing."

Even though our spirit is instantaneously reconciled with God and is plugged into the Tree of Life, our soul (mind, will and emotions) aren't immediately plugged in. However, our soul craves for that life and relationship.

In order to fill the void and emptiness in our soul, sometimes our mind will do things to medicate itself like find addictions and strongholds thinking these things will bring life to the soul. It's like we're on a branch of good or evil trying to find life.

God's Word holds the key to enable us to move from the Tree of the Knowledge of Good and Evil to the Tree of Life. However, it is extremely important to understand that we must study God's Word for more than just obtaining "knowledge of God." We must read His Word for "relationship." The Scribes and Pharisees of Jesus' day fell into this trap. They possessed an exorbitant amount of knowledge related to the Law, yet they were void of a genuine relationship with God. In fact, Jesus even referred to them as "hypocrites" in Matthew 23:27 (NIV). He went on to say to the teachers of the law and the Pharisees in that same verse, "You are like whitewashed tombs, which look beautiful on the outside but on the inside are full of the bones of the dead and everything unclean." They had a great deal of knowledge, but their knowledge was void of a relationship with the God they so vigorously studied.

Christians today face the same fate if we fail to walk in the loving and fulfilling relationship to which we are called by God Himself. If we seek God by studying and for the sake of knowledge alone, who is in control? We are. Instead, we should read to "listen" and to "build relationship" with Him.

We need to actively listen and then "surrender" to what he is saying to us. Then, God is in control.

If the only way to heal and be more like Christ is by study and knowledge, then the only ones who can have victory would be the "A" students. Instead we are to have faith like a child: "And he said: 'Truly I tell you, unless you change and become like little children, you will never enter the kingdom of heaven'" (Matthew 18:3 NIV). He lifts up those that are humble and those that listen, trust and follow: "The greatest among you will be your servant" (Matthew 23:11 NIV). When we learn to read the Bible for the purpose of expanding our relationship with our Heavenly Father, we find that we don't have to "try harder" to live an abundant Christian life. Instead, it just comes naturally because we are connected to the power source.

We must study God's Word for more than just obtaining "knowledge of God", we must read His word for "relationship".

Chapter 4

Understanding Why We Are Broken

We need a "relationship" with God if we are going to be healed or even recognize our brokenness. Jesus made this very clear as he instructed the disciples. In John 15 he basically said to them, "Apart from me, you can't do this." His literal words were: "I am the vine; you are the branches. If you remain in me and I in you, you will bear much fruit; apart from me you can do nothing" (John 15:5 NIV). The reality is that when we are connected to Jesus and Jesus is connected to us, we will bear the fruit of the Christian life. Jesus invites us to walk with Him in victory and in the abundant life.

God's plan for us is to be free! We no longer have to be enslaved to our old way of thinking and living. Romans 6:6 says it like this, "For we know that our old self was crucified with Him so that the body of sin might be done away with that we should no longer be slaves to sin" (NIV). This is great news! We no longer have to be under the insidious rule of sin!

In Philippians 2:12-13 we are told to "work out our own salvation." It says, "Therefore, my dear friends, as you have always obeyed – not only in my presence, but now much more in my absence – continue to work out your salvation with fear and trembling, for it is God who works in you to will and to act in order to fulfill his good purpose" (NIV). Notice it says to "work out" your salvation, I'm so glad it doesn't say, "work for" your salvation.

We have already established that when we accept Jesus as our Lord and Savior, our spirit is instaniously made new. That has already happened. So, our spirit doesn't need to be "worked out." But what needs to be "worked out" is our heart, our woundedness, our brokenness, our emotions and our will. That is our very soul. We must allow the Holy Spirit to "re-wire" our heart and soul with His truth.

The million-dollar question then becomes, "How do we 'work out our salvation' as it pertains to our soul (mind, will and emotions)?" In order to answer that question we must first understand some things about how amazingly powerful our minds have been created. Our mind and our neurological system have amazing capabilities.

To restate the problem: When we come to Christ, the old nature dies and is buried with Christ. However, that old nature, that spirit of woundedness and darkness that controlled our life before Christ, already programmed our mind for us. That's why when we wake up the next day after accepting Jesus as the Lord of our life, even though our spirit is now new, our body, mind and neurosystem is wired to the "old" nature and it's amazing how powerful it can be of convincing us of things that are not true.

40

Our mind and our neurosystem can actually convince us that a lie is true. Even though the Scriptures make it very clear that we are a "new creation" in Christ, our mind (and often the enemy of our soul) will try to convince us otherwise.

The truth is, we have "become the righteousness of God" according to 2 Corinthians 5:21. However, we believe the lie and "feel" guilt, shame and condemnation. Again, the truth as declared by the Word of God is that "God made Him who had no sin to be sin for us, so that in Him we might become the righteousness of God" (2 Corinthians 5:21 NIV). Yet, our mind will make us "feel" like we are not the righteousness of God. In fact, we may feel overwhelmed with guilt and heartache.

To show you the power of this truth let me share with you the documented experiences of a friend of mine who was an amputee. Amputees develop a condition called Phantom Limb Syndrome. There have been countless examples of individuals, like my friend who have had their leg removed from the knee down. Even though the leg was cut off, the person's foot would still itch even though there is no foot there. The mind is saying, "My foot itches," and it creates anxiety in the patient because they can't scratch their foot because it's not there.

So doctors determined that if the mind thinks the foot itches, let's give it Benadryl to see what happens. After taking Benadryl, the itching sensation would go away. However, the same sensation would come back. By medicating and reinforcing the lie, the lie would continue to exist. There would be times of relief and times of pain or itching; more times of relief followed by times of pain or itching. This scenario just continued to repeat itself as long as the symptoms were being treated with Benadryl. Now, instead of prescribing Benadryl to these patients, doctors will take something like a Brillo pad and begin to scrub the area of the stub where the nerve endings are to tell the brain that it is no longer the middle of the leg, but it is now the end of the leg.

Through this simple treatment, the phantom pain is short-lived and will eventually completely disappear. It's amazing that our mind has that much influence to convince someone that their foot itches when there isn't anything there. In order to resolve the problem the brain and nerve system had to be retrained or rewired to align with the truth.

Something very similar happens to us on a spiritual level. We go through a "spiritual surgery" of sorts in that Jesus takes away our sin and sets our spirit free. However, our soul (mind, will and emotions) is still wired to think that we need to carry all the emotional pain and hurts that, in a very real spiritual sense, don't even exist any longer. They were taken care of at the cross.

However, when Christians struggle with brokenness, so many religions simply say, "Try harder" or "Do this or do that." Their instruction, as sincere as it may be, just deals with the symptoms by providing "spiritual Benadryl" rather than dealing with the lie. As a result those struggling in their Christian walk have good days followed by bad days; good days, followed by bad days. They live out the "clean diaper, dirty diaper" analogy spoken of earlier. They go from clean diaper to dirty diaper and keep repeating the process without experiencing the opportunity to mature in their faith to the point of actually overcoming this syndrome and experiencing complete healing.

But there is hope! There is an alternative to just "trying harder!" When we "renew" our mind according to Romans 12:2 and seek healing from God, a "rewiring" of this system referred to as our soul (mind, will and emotions) takes place to match the new spirit that has been created within us. When this happens, the abundant life God promises us can then be experienced.

So, what keeps us from walking healed and whole in our soul in similar fashion to our spirit? A significant reason why people continue to live a life of brokenness, even though their spirit is healed and they are on their way to heaven, is because for every mile of country road there are two miles of ditches. There is the "Keep Trying Harder" ditch and the "There's No Hope" ditch. The enemy doesn't care which ditch he puts you in because his purpose is to keep you off the path God wants you on. He'll put you in this ditch that says, "You're okay, you're fine, there are people worse than you. All you have to do is try harder and you'll get there."

Or he'll put you in another ditch that causes you to say, "There's no hope for me" and "This is just the way I am." Other versions of this ditch sound like:

- "I've always been this way."
- "I've always been a yeller."
- "My mom was depressed; my dad was depressed, my grandmother was depressed. It's just the way it is and it's who we are and there isn't anything that can change."
- "There's no hope for this relationship."
- "These habits are just who I am and there's no hope."
- "There's no hope for who I am."

After lying in one of these ditches for a period of time we begin to believe the lie that we truly can't change. It's as though we have been blinded to the truth or there is something covering our spiritual eyes preventing us from acting on the truth God has already established for our lives. However, the good news is that the "veil" that causes us to continue in brokenness can be lifted. 2 Corinthians 3:16-17 (NIV) tells us very clearly, "But whenever anyone turns to the Lord, the veil is taken away. Now the Lord is the Spirit, and where the Spirit of the Lord is, there is freedom."

When it comes to the subject of freedom, there are two types of people: Those trapped in bondage and those set free from bondage. Thankfully, our Heavenly Father set a plan in motion through His Son so we don't have to stay trapped. One of the greatest illustrations I have found to illustrate the subtleness, yet profoundness, of this subject came from the diary of one of the world renowned magicians who stunned audiences on multiple continents with his amazing talents and illusions.

In a biography of Harry Houdini, the great escape artist back in the early 1900's, an account from his personal diary is disclosed that no one knew about until after his death when his personal journal was discovered. It is very well known that Houdini would always accept outrageous challenges to prove that he was the world's greatest escape artist. One of his greatest tests came when he was dared to free himself from a brand new prison being built in London that had the latest technology of its time and was considered escape proof. The civic leaders thought there was no better way to test their new facility than to have the world's greatest escape artist try to escape from it. It was the challenge of the century and Harry Houdini couldn't resist the opportunity. He thought this would surely be recorded as one of the greatest stunts in history and would be a shining star to his already prestigious legacy.

To sell out the theater, he told people to come to the show because he was going to be locked in this escape-proof prison in the morning and would escape in time to be at the theater to perform his evening show. The place was a sellout. However, no one was there to see his show, but they were there to see if he was going to walk out on that stage after being locked up in an inescapable prison cell.

Houdini indicated in his journal that when he was taken to the cell the guards took great precaution to make sure he wasn't smuggling in anything to pick the lock. However, they didn't know that Houdini had the ability to swallow picks that he could use later and prior to his incarceration he had swallowed some lock picks to be used later. The guards then, as an extra precaution, took any article of clothing they suspected he could use in his escape attempt and locked them in a different area. After taking all the precautions the guards left him alone in the jail cell.

Houdini explained in his journal that after the guards left he coughed up the picks, reached through the bars and began trying to pick the lock. Since he was behind the bars he was not able to see what he was doing, so he listened intently to the tumblers as he tried to get them to fall into place. He kept working on the lock and kept working on the lock, but he couldn't get the tumblers to fall into place.

Minutes eventually turned to hours in his effort to escape and he became physically and mentally exhausted. He confessed in his journal that he began to break out in a sweat as he envisioned headlines in the newspapers the next day saying, "World's Greatest Escape Artist Fails." He realized he was getting closer to his evening performance time and he wasn't going to be there. After hours of exhausting effort, he gave up.

Then, as his forehead leaned on the cell door in exhaustion, the door opened. He then realized that in the guards' efforts to make sure he didn't have any tricks up his sleeve; they forgot to lock the cell door. All those hours Houdini was trying to unlock a door that wasn't even locked.

So, here's the question that this story so vividly illustrates, "What makes a prisoner?" Is it one that is locked in a cell or is it, one that just simply believes the door is locked? As believers, many walk in that state of brokenness thinking there's no hope. The enemy realizes that through Christ the door has been unlocked so the captives can be set free. But his goal is still the same – to convince you of the lie that says, "You are a prisoner; you are still locked in a cell." Many Christians today sit as prisoners in unlocked cells.

How do we answer that lie and how do we find the truth? How do we come to a place where we're not just functional and getting by, but we are truly healed and transformed in our hearts the same way our spirit is healed and transformed? It is simply by understanding, accepting, believing and acting on the truth God has already given to us in His Word. The Bible is full of truths that will change and transform you from "just getting by" to living the "abundant life" God intends for you to live.

Jesus said in Luke 4:18 (NKJV), "The Spirit of the Lord is upon me...to proclaim liberty to the captives" and 1 John 4:4 (NKJV) declares, "...greater is He that is in you, than he that is in the world." Jesus is still proclaiming to each of us today that He is still available to liberate those that are captive (or think they are captive)! We must understand that the One that is *in* us as believers is greater than the enemy that would try to make us believe the lie of hopelessness and the lie that we are destined to live in brokenness.

Take a moment right now to ask your Heavenly Father the following questions; then take time to listen to His response to you. Yes, God wants to speak directly and very personally to you. Ask Him:

- "Father, what is one word you would say to describe how You see me?"

- "Father, is there a lie that I have believed in that you want to show me?"

- "Father, what is your truth that should replace this lie I have believed?"

- "Father, your Word, which is truth says " I am a new creation, the old is gone, behold all is new." What does that mean to me personally?

Signs of Brokenness

Dr. Derek Prince, in his book, "Blessings and Curses," looks to Deuteronomy 28 to show there are 28 signs of brokenness described there. One or many of these 28 signs may be in a person's life to which God can bring healing and restoration. He doesn't want you to live in any of these "prison cells." Rather, He wants you to live in total freedom from these potential schemes or the enemy. **(Keep in mind, we can all have "rough" moments in life when some of these may occur and that doesn't mean you're "broken." But these describe how a broken person actually defines and lives their life.)**

1. God Seems Distant. (You think your personal wounds, hurts and brokenness are not of that much concern to God.)

2. God Seems Angry. (Some people think God is just waiting for them to mess up so He can bring down His judgment.)
3. Difficulty having a dynamic faith.
4. Difficulty walking in agape love (unconditional love). – Do you put conditions on love? For example, "when I'm good, then God loves me."
5. Difficulty reading and understanding Scripture.
6. Difficulty grasping spiritual truths.
7. Absence of self love and feeling a sense of unworthiness. (You feel you aren't worthy, have a low self image, and believe lies about yourselves, then project that image on God. This results in believing God thinks you aren't worthy and, therefore, must not love you.)
8. Inability to give and receive love.
9. Tendency towards strife.
10. Self-rejection and negative talk. (You may joke negatively about yourself saying things like, "I'm so stupid" and "You probably don't want to hang out with me because I'm such a loser" simply to stir a response.)
11. Difficulty forgiving people.
12. Fatalism and declaring a loss of control in life.
13. Inner vows that decree control and determination to reach a "preferred future" by willpower. (An "inner vow" is simply telling myself, "I'm going to be the god of this portion of my life and I won't allow Jesus to have control of that part of my life." If you have ever been betrayed by a person such as someone cheating on you in a relationship, it's easy to put up walls and not let anyone get close to you so they don't have an

opportunity to hurt you. "Fool me once, shame on you; fool me twice, shame on me." Inner vows build walls that are designed for protection, but become a prison cell.)

14. Avoidance of intimacy with loved ones.
15. Lack of financial wisdom. (This reveals itself as being perpetually in financial debt and stress which comes from an orphan spirit of trying to get things to make sure you're not lacking anything; it happens simply because of not understanding the truth and promises of God.)
16. Expecting sickness.
17. Difficulty coping with people in authority over you.
18. Inward pain.
19. Spirit of heaviness or depression.
20. Overemphasis on works and accomplishments. (This is an indicator that we are trying to prove our worth or value.)
21. Overemphasis on rules.
22. Tendency toward sexual uncleanness.
23. Tendency toward addictions.
24. Obsessiveness with natural needs such as sleep, food, exercise and cleanliness.
25. Strong fears, rebellion, hatred and arrogance.
26. Lack of people skills.
27. Inability to deal with the death of loved ones.
28. Pride and an absence of the fear of the Lord.

Take a moment right now to allow God to speak to you about any of the "Signs of Brokenness" listed above.

First, tell God you desire to hear from Him by saying this: "Father, I'm giving you permission to speak into my heart; I'm surrendering to you."

Second, ask God this: "Father, are there one or two items (or more) from which you desire to heal me and set me free?"

"What makes a prisoner?
One who sits in a locked cell or one who simply thinks the
door is locked?"

Chapter 5

Levels of Change – Levels 1-3

Have you ever pondered the question, "Why did Jesus come to earth?" Your immediate answer is probably the same as most Christians, "To give us eternal life." While that is very true, there is actually more to His purpose of invading humanity with His divine presence.

Early in the book of Luke Jesus begins his ministry and purpose on earth by reading out of Isaiah: "The Spirit of the Lord is upon Me, because He has anointed Me to preach the gospel to the poor; He has sent Me to heal the brokenhearted, to proclaim liberty to the captives and recovery of sight to the blind; to set at liberty those who are oppressed; to proclaim the acceptable year of the Lord." (Luke 4:18-19 NKJV)

Yes, Jesus came to give us eternal life. But He also came to give us victory in our lives while we are on earth. God desires that we live a life of spiritual triumph while on our journey through this lifetime. He desires to "heal the brokenhearted!" He desires to "liberate the captives!" He desires to give "sight to the blind!" He desires to "free the oppressed!"

As I alluded to earlier, in the midst of this struggle and turmoil we call "life," we develop an erroneous "potty training" kind of theology by thinking, "Jesus died on the cross for my sins and my messes and my life is a never-ending cycle of sinning and coming to Jesus for forgiveness."

Thankfully, there eventually comes a point in every parent's life where you don't have to change the diaper any longer – this is transformation. The child goes through that glorious "potty training" stage and they learn they no longer have to make the messes that require the proverbial "cleanup." A transformation occurs in their lifestyle. Something changes that makes the past issues and the way they dealt with them non-relevant.

How many tree houses have you built in the Tree of the Knowledge of Good and Evil? How many hurts and wounds have you not entrusted to God for complete healing?

The process to receive God's healing, liberation and freedom for our soul (mind, will and emotions) involves navigating through effective change or "working out our salvation" as Philippians 2:12 states. There are essentially five levels of change through which we typically navigate. Some of these levels of change have much more effectiveness than others. Some levels involve the futile attempt of us trying to heal ourselves, while two of them require God to intervene. Let's examine these five levels together. The first three levels of change are ways we try to deal with our hurts on our own apart from Christ.

First Level of Change – Environmental Change

Environmental change is the "easiest" option to try to escape pain in our lives. However, it is also woefully ineffective. Statements such as the following are evidence environmental change:

- "The reason I'm sad is because of you."
- "The reason I have a problem is because of you."
- "I would be happy if I wasn't in a relationship with this person."
- "I would be happy if I wasn't married to this person."
- "I would be happy if it wasn't for my job."
- "I would be happy if it wasn't for my boss."
- "I would be happy if it wasn't for where I live."
- "I would be happy if I could have a family or someone in my life."
- "I would be happy if I could find a nicer home."

In this level of change we begin to think the answer to our problems is somewhere in our environment. So we leave a relationship because we're convinced we would be happy if it wasn't for the other person.

The problem is that after we leave that relationship, marriage, or church, at the end of the day, we're still stuck with ourselves and that's where the brokenness lies.

Environment change looks outward and blames everyone and everything else. The person active in this level of change believes a lie something like this: The reason they were divorced five times or were fired from eight different jobs wasn't because they have a problem... it was because everyone else was a jerk. At this level one can easily self-justify and become the victim, focusing on the speck of dust in the other person's eye and never looking at the plank that's in their own eye as Matthew 7:5 (NKJV) so appropriately states: "Hypocrite! First remove the plank from your own eye, and then you will see clearly to remove the speck from your brother's eye." This person is not only quick to judge, but they are experts at blaming others, thereby diverting the attention away from the real issue, themselves.

Levels of change two and three start looking inward and recognize that there may be a problem within "me." Although this is a good step, it also has its traps and limitations.

Second Level of Change – Behavioral Change

The second level of change, Behavioral Change, is the way we act and try to behave based on our thoughts and feelings. We fall into this trap a lot. That is, we think being a Christian is about controlling oneself and exhibiting good behavior. The thinking in this level of change is that if we act "good," we will be a good Christian. It becomes all about our behavior and we focus on that almost exclusively.

People who center on this process of change will say things like…

- "I'm going to try harder to not look at the things on the internet that I shouldn't be looking at."

- "I'm going to try harder not to yell at my kids."

- "I'm going to try harder not to have an addiction to food (or TV or exercise or whatever it is that I'm using to help me escape from my pain)."

The next two levels (levels three and four) of change are where modern counseling and much religion will focus, and this is a great time to compare and contrast how the fifth level of change is vastly different. Let me first say, I am a huge believer in good Christian counseling. I firmly believe it's vital to unpacking situations in life. I will say it again; I am 100% in favor of using good Christian counseling.

But secular counseling (and even some "Christian" counseling and religion) has its limitations. Much of what secular counseling has to offer deals with levels two and three of the Levels of Change. The two main resources used are Cognitive Behavioral Therapy and Rational Emotive Therapy.

Cognitive Behavioral Therapy guides you to "think your way to a better behavior" by using your mind to control your behavior.

This modality suggests you can simply tell yourself happy truths or thoughts.

We can sometimes give this a Christian version and simply find a verse and just "name it and claim it." While confessing God's word is a good thing (in fact, it's a great thing), we can sometimes leave the relational element with our Father out of the scripture much like what the Pharisees did and it then becomes more academic than life-giving. We will talk more about hearing God and how to stand on God's word in levels four and five. There is also an entire chapter later in this book devoted to "Hearing God."

The second popular modality in counseling is Rational Emotive Therapy. This is the theory or belief that when you think rational thoughts you will have rational emotions that lead to rational behavior. While this seems to have merit and make sense, it is missing a very important component in the way we were created. It is again placing the focus on oneself as the healer, rather than relying on the Creator for healing. Relying on just your own ability and willpower to fix yourself and making the main component of change behavior oriented is like arm wrestling yourself. Who's winning? You are. Who's losing? You are. There are good days and there are bad days. There are days of "clean diapers" and there are days of "dirty diapers."

We then boil our faith down to our behavior and say, "When my behavior is 'good,' God is happy with me, but once I fail God is unhappy with me and I have to go to Him for forgiveness." That is why many Christians feel "unloved" by God and "unworthy" of salvation when they fail. The truth is

58

that God doesn't love us any differently when we fail. But, when we believe a lie from the enemy, it's hard, and I believe even impossible, to deal with it solely on a behavior level.

Third Level of Change – Capability or Willpower to Change

The third level of change, Capability or Willpower to Change says, "Might makes right!" and "Pull Harder!" (from the aforementioned lawn mower illustration) and "Dig in!" God gave us willpower and capabilities and those things are good things. But when we try to fix ourselves apart from Him, it's not a good option.

If you've ever tried to lose weight, you will understand this level. The first five pounds is usually pretty easy. The second five pounds is a bit more difficult. By the time you are trying to hit that 15 pound mark you're fighting for every pound. You're using your own capabilities. You're using your own willpower. You're saying, "I'm not going to eat that chocolate." And you say that through sheer determination. After you've lost that 15 or 18 pounds something happens. It's like a rubber band that's overextended and something snaps; instead of losing that 15 or 25 pounds, you gain an extra 5 or 10 pounds and you're worse off than when you started. You go on a binge because you were trying to lose weight based on your capabilities and your behavior. Then you feel defeated.

Whatever we have our focus on we prioritize our entire life around. If we focus on our problem being something in our environment or our behavior or our capabilities, then we shape our entire life around that. In contrast, the Bible tells us in Matthew 6:33 (NIV), "Seek first the Kingdom of God." We have to quit seeking solutions when we need to seek **relationship**.

The rest of this verse and the following verse reveals even more truth. It says, "But seek first His Kingdom and His righteousness, and all these things will be given to you as well. Therefore do not worry about tomorrow, for tomorrow will worry about itself. Each day has enough trouble of its own" (Matthew 6:33-34 NIV). Tomorrow has enough problems; I don't need to go around adding to it. The problem department is full. No need to look for more.

Don't let your focus be your problem, but follow the advice of the Scripture and "seek first the Kingdom of God." Then everything in your life will be built around that focus of relationship with your Heavenly Father.

As was mentioned previously, the first three levels of change we have influence over. However, to have a change at levels four and five, God has to speak. He has to show up. In these levels you will see that need to hear God's voice in order to be transformed.

The broken heart cannot be healed until the spirit is healed.

Chapter 6

Fourth Level of Change –

Belief-Based Change

As we established in the previous chapter regarding the first three levels of change, Environmental Change looks outward and blames everyone and everything else. Behavioral Change looks at changing our behavior and by acting better we believe things will improve. And last, Capability or Willpower to Change indicates all we have to do is keep trying and keep pulling harder as if by brute force we will overcome the brokenness in our lives. This now leads us to the fourth level of change where we actually have to begin to look to and depend on God to resolve our pain rather than focusing on our own abilities.

Fourth Level of Change – Belief-Based Change

At this level God needs to be involved. This is when we finally come to the realization that lasting and effective change and transformation can't happen unless we're in a relationship with God. This is where we distinguish the vast difference between thought and belief.

Let's look again at the words of Jesus when He launched His earthly ministry in Luke 4:18-19 (NKJV): "The Spirit of the Lord is upon Me, because He has anointed Me to preach the gospel to the poor; He has sent me to heal the brokenhearted, to proclaim liberty to the captives and recovery of sight to the blind; to set at liberty those who are oppressed; to proclaim the acceptable year of the Lord."

As we have already established, the broken heart cannot be healed until the spirit is healed. Only after the spirit is healed, can the broken heart or soul (mind, will and emotions) be healed. And Jesus is the only one who can heal a broken heart.

There are other things that will help us cope with life, such as medication and counseling, but these things don't bring healing, they simply allow us to function. They are meant to be "that spare donut tire" that gets us to a place where real change can take place. The reality is that Jesus is the only one that can heal your broken heart and He has come to do just that.

To experience healing, it is vitally important to first understand the difference between a *thought* and a *belief*. The mixing of these two concepts has brought a lot of confusion to Christians. Let's look at the difference between these two elements.

A thought is in your mind and it's very conscious. Here is a simple example of a thought: "Tomorrow I'm going to mow the lawn." You can see it is very tangible, easy to identify and easy to change.

In contrast, a belief is something much deeper than a thought. It is something that you can't quite describe. It's a feeling. It's an unction. There are no words to attach to it because it is more like an conviction.

Here is another important distinction between these two components. **A thought is in the mind, but a belief resides in the heart.** For example, since we have freedom in our nation, some people think they will participate by voting, but 50% of people in our country don't vote because it's only a thought. However, if you ask a Marine (or any service man or woman) how he or she feels about freedom, you will discover it's not a thought, but a belief. Their belief is so strong that they are willing to give their life for it.

Here is a very simple way to tell the difference between a thought and a belief. When you hear God's truth and you respond with, "Yeah, but…" or "I know, but…," That is a thought rather than a belief. For example, often people who are in an inappropriate relationship will say, "I know what the Bible says, but…." They are not really believing in their heart that what the Word of God says is in their best interest and that God will be faithful. The knowledge may be in their brain, but the revelation of that truth is not in their heart. So now the scripture that talks about not being unequally yoked is just a thought and not a belief.

We need to recognize important "thought" phrases, such as, "I know, but…," so that we are cognizant of it when we say those things. The Bible tells us to "take every thought captive to make it obedient to Christ" (2 Corinthians 10:5 NIV). Part of "taking every thought captive" is recognizing the lie, "I know, but...." We must recognize it as a thought which means "I have a belief that is not in alignment with the Word of God." We then must replace the lie with the truth of God's Word and put the truth in our heart. If I ever say something like, "I know, but...," then I can take steps to bring that thought into captivity, then find the truth and make the truth part of my belief system.

A belief drives you, it defines you, it's who you are and you will give your life to it; you will give up things for it and make sacrifices. A belief is so deep that you will ask the question, "Am I willing to lay my life down for that belief?" Matthew 16:24 (NIV) addresses this subject: "Then Jesus said to his disciples, 'If anyone would come after me, he must deny himself and take up his cross and follow me.'"

Our thoughts and beliefs aren't always in alignment. What often takes place is a "tug of war" for what our flesh wants against what God's Spirit is leading us to do. God is trying to lead us to a place of healing if we will trust him.

Beliefs are also obscure at times. Have you ever been in a "funk" and you don't know why? Or have you ever felt depressed without knowing why? If you have ever dealt with anyone who is depressed, you may ask them why they are depressed and then say something like, "But, look at all the good things in your life." And they respond, "I know, but I'm still depressed." You are trying to communicate with them on a thinking level when they are experiencing something at the belief level.

66

Thinking deals with the mind and belief deals with the heart. Proverbs 23:7 (AMP) says, "As a man thinks in his heart, so is he." I *know* I'm blessed, I *know* God is able to heal, I *know* I should be happy.

But as you "think in your heart" or as you *believe* in your heart, so are you. It does not say, "As you think in your mind." It says, "As you think in your heart" or, in other words, "As you believe in your heart, so are you."

In Romans 10:9 it says, "If you confess with your mouth and 'believe' in your heart (not in your mind) that Jesus is Lord, you will be saved." By putting God's truth in our heart it renewed our spirit. The same principle applies to renewing our soul. It will take place over time because the heart and soul are different elements of how we have been created. **But, just like when our spirit was transformed, the moment we get God's truth into our heart that area of our soul becomes transformed.** This is the very heart of the message of this book. Transformation and healing of our brokenness will only come as God's truth goes from being an intellectual thought to a dynamic belief. Again, it is when "…we take captive every thought to make it obedient to Christ" (2 Corinthians 10:5 NIV). In its simplest definition, healing the broken heart occurs when we allow the Holy Spirit to replace the lies the enemy wants us to hold on to with the truth of God's Word.

Negative beliefs or lies are detrimental to your spiritual wellbeing. A negative belief is indicated when you say things like, "I feel stupid" or "I feel like a failure." These thoughts and "feelings" may seem real, but are contrary to the way your heavenly Father sees you. They will continue to influence your life until you take them captive.

This is why it is so important to know and understand the Word of God because if we don't know God's truth or if we allow lies to go unchallenged and to take root in our minds as a thought, it will then move into our heart to become a belief. All beliefs begin as a thought and move into our heart to become a belief.

There are times we know we should believe certain things, but they seem to be just a thought. For example, we know we should be happy, blessed, victorious, etc. We "know" these things, but we don't feel or believe these things. For some reason these thoughts have not been adopted into our belief system. This begs the question, "How do we change our thoughts and beliefs?"

How to Change Your Thoughts and Beliefs

There are two ways to change a thought and a belief; whether it's getting the wrong belief out of your heart or getting a truth of God that is only a thought and making it a belief.

The first way to change a thought or belief is preventive. Just simply don't allow the lie to enter your thoughts or your beliefs (heart). In Proverbs 4:23 (NIV) we are told, "Above all else, guard your heart, for everything you do flows from it." Your heart (or belief) is where the issues of life come from. What are you watching? What are you listening to? What influences are you letting in? Granted, we can't live in a bubble, nor are we to isolate ourselves from the world. But, we do need to guard our hearts and take captive any thought that doesn't line up with the Word of God.

The issues of life come from our heart, but so many times we try to deal with it on a thinking level. But "thinking" is not the problem; it's the belief that is at the core of the issue. When you see the difference between a thought and a belief, you will realize how important it is to guard your heart.

Regardless of what is real, whatever is in the heart is what you will do or how you will behave. If the devil can get a lie into your heart, it doesn't matter what your brain thinks about a promise. According to Proverbs 4:23 we live our lives based on what we believe in our heart. That's why it tells us to "guard our heart" at all costs.

While raising three boys, we would watch television together in the evening like many families. Whenever anything questionable appeared on the screen or if an inappropriate commercial suddenly appeared, my wife would always tell our young boys, "Guard your heart." And each of them would put their hands over their eyes so they wouldn't see what was on television. Rather than telling them not to look, they learned the importance of "guarding their heart." On one occasion, one of the boys said, "You know, you can usually tell by the music when you need to guard your heart." Yes, we had a very observant boy we were raising.

The eyes and the ears are a window to the mind and the mind is a window to the heart. In Matthew 6:22 (NIV) Jesus said, "The eye is the lamp of the body." What we watch and listen to gets into our mind, then into our heart and creates a belief system. It may sound trite in our current culture, but the absolute truth is that what you read and listen to determines what you believe. Romans 10:17 tells us that "Faith comes from hearing…." Interestingly, our lack of faith can also come from "hearing" the wrong things.

The second way to change a thought and a belief is to take the thought captive. This involves recognizing those things in our thoughts and our beliefs that are contrary to the Word of God, understanding them to be lies, and then replacing them with the truth based on the Word of God.

How do we clean out the junk or lies that are already in our mind and our heart? We need to take captive every thought. It is important to repeat the truth of 2 Corinthians 10:5 (NIV), "We demolish arguments and every pretension that sets itself up against the knowledge of God, and we take captive every thought to make it obedient to Christ."

The word "captive," in the original Greek language, literally meant to take a spear and jab it into someone's back. When a Roman soldier took a prisoner captive, he would jab the prisoner in the back with the spear to keep them moving forward. They would parade their captives down through town to show victory. So to take "captive" was to force them to obey their instruction.

In this same manner, the Bible tells us to "take every thought captive" and we use the Word of God as the spear or "Sword" to keep every thought in line. So when a thought comes to our mind like "you're ugly," "you're stupid," or "you're a failure," we need to recognize that as a thought that is not based on the Word of God and take it captive by jabbing it in the back and making it submit and leave your mind. We can't afford to allow those kinds of thoughts to bounce around in our mind, or affirm itself, or take root in our mind.

So, with every thought I'm going to ask myself, "Is this truth? Does it line up with God's truth? Or is it a lie, and is it contrary to God's word? We need to recognize the lies of the enemy. It's amazing to me that people have a hard time believing God can speak to them; that He can literally speak into their hearts. Yet it's easy to believe that the devil speaks such things as, "You're fat, you're a loser, you're going to fail." God doesn't speak those things to your mind. Sometimes there is a bit of truth in a lie from the enemy. That's what makes it believable.

Let me ask you this simple question, are we meant to have a "relationship" with Jesus? Yes, we are. Is it possible to have a relationship if there's no communication? NO. The whole purpose of Christ coming to earth, dying on the cross, and rising from the dead is so we can once again communicate and have a relationship with Him. He has, He does, and He will speak to you in a way that you can hear Him. The Bible says, "My sheep hear my voice" (John 10:27 NKJV). God wants to speak to the broken heart.

We need to recognize other sources of lies. The enemy can use some of the people in your life to speak lies into your mind.

You may have heard this statement before, "Hurt people hurt people" or "Hurting people hurt people." Usually when someone inflicts pain into your life through their words or actions you will find their assault toward you is a result of the pain they are trying to deal with in their own life.

The enemy can also use things that we see, read and hear to distort the truth in our minds (television, movies, music, magazines, books). We need to be able to recognize the lie and then take those thoughts captive and say, "Those words don't line up with the Word of God."

It is important to understand that your source of truth isn't what you experience. Instead, your source of truth is the Word of God. That's why it's necessary to read the Word of God consistently, so you know the truth and can quickly identify a lie. Jesus said in John 8:32 (NKJV), "And you shall know the truth, and the truth shall make you free."

Knowing the Word of God will enable you to not conform to the patterns of the enemy and will allow God to transform your mind. We are instructed in this way in Romans 12:2 (NIV): "Do not conform to the pattern of this world, but be transformed by the renewing of your mind." We "renew our mind" on the Word of God.

Do you remember the amputee and the phantom limb syndrome discussed earlier in this book? It is very common for an amputee to experience a sensation in a limb that no longer is attached to their body because their mind was programmed to associate that specific feeling with the limb that is no longer attached. In the same way, before God saved us, the old nature was able to speak some stupid and crazy lies to our mind. Now we have to renew our minds by the Word of God and replace all the lies that were put in there before we discovered Jesus.

If we're simply reading a verse from the Bible every other day or once a week, but we're listening to depressing news and the gossip of our friends and all the junk that's out there, is it any wonder that we lose this battle? In fact, I would say if we aren't using any filters and we aren't seeking Godly advice, eventually we will lose our desire to even read God's word and be with Him.

Have you ever changed the filter in your furnace and found it to be really bad? It's very dirty, gross and disgusting. When the filter gets that dirty, there is dust that constantly accumulates in the house. But when you change the filter, it prevents the dust from coming through the heating ducts. In the same way, we need to change the filter (and keep it clean) that filters every thought that comes into our mind. The Word of God is what constantly cleanses that filter to protect our mind.

An unprotected or unfiltered mind is fertile ground for the deception of the enemy. Even as a Christian, you can get caught up in a lie or a set of lies that will thrust you into what I term, "The Cycle of a Stronghold." In the next chapter we will discuss in detail the destructive nature of this syndrome and how to break free from it.

God's truth will always be found in His Word.

Chapter 7

The Cycle of a Stronghold

As was illustrated in the aforementioned story about Harry Houdini, because we still believe the jail cell door is locked and we are prisoners or victims, we enter into a cycle and self-destructive pattern that causes us to think even when things are working out for our good that it's too good to be true and we do something to sabotage it. That is, we fall into an emotional and spiritual trap that continues to spiral downward as we hold on for dear life. Let me explain how this process works and how its cyclical nature is perpetuated like a merry-go-round out of control.

The Cycle of a Stronghold first begins with an event which is often a negative experience. This experience can take on many forms and may involve other people. It is something that happens to you either by self-infliction or it may be something that happened to you as a result of someone else's actions. Whatever the circumstances may have been, you experience wounds, pain or some type of distress as a result.

After the negative experience, there's a lie that's attached to it. In this cycle your source of truth becomes the situation and the lie instead of the Word of God. You believe the lie that you're not worthy; no one wants you; you're not deserving, etc. These thoughts and feelings overtake you and infiltrate your belief system.

That lie then triggers defense mechanisms in our lives to protect ourselves and we make inner vows. You will begin saying things that you think will protect you based on the lie you believed. You will hear yourself say things like, "I will never trust anyone again" or "I will never get close to anyone again" or "I'm completely done with relationships." You may also react through addictions or other coping mechanisms.

Then people will react and respond to what we say and do. As people respond to your negative behavior it will result in additional hurt and pain being inflicted on you resulting in the same pattern repeating itself over and over again. This creates a vicious cycle of brokenness in your life and you become self-destructive in your habits, sabotaging the very things God wants for you. The lie then becomes more real and stronger than it ever was before.

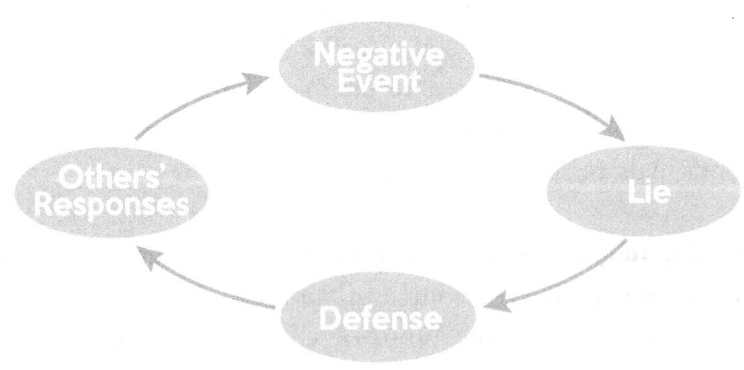

Breaking The Cycle of a Stronghold

So just how does one get off this crazy circular horror ride and break free from The Cycle of a Stronghold? "Religion" and secular psychiatry would likely tell you to tear down the defensive response, to deal with the behavior. But your behavior isn't the core problem. So, dealing with your behavior may help some, but it won't resolve the real issue. Dealing with your behavior can be a coping mechanism, but it's not the full answer. How do you go from just coping with life to breaking the cycle of the stronghold(s) you experience so you can walk in the abundant life Jesus has planned for you? What is the real problem and how do you break free?

You have to go back to the lie, confront it, and deal with this Cycle of a Stronghold at its systemic point of origin. You confront the lie with truth. When you know the truth, the truth will set you free.

This cycle and how to break from it was demonstrated in a very powerful way by an attendee in one of our first Living Free Classes. For the purposes of this story we'll just call this person "Mike." Mike, a local college student, was one of the most cynical people I had met and was very skeptical about God being able to "talk" to a person. After the class he came to me seeking advice.

He said, "I'm pretty much an 'A' student. Last week I got a B+ on a quiz and it really upset me. The more I thought about it, the more upset I became, even to a point that I thought to myself, 'why is this bothering me so much?' Pastor, why do you think it bothers me so much?"

My response to him was, "Did you ask Father?" "No," came his quick response. I then encouraged him, "Next time you are alone with God, just ask Him, 'Father, why is this bothering me so much?'" My suggestion was met with a rolling of the eyes and a non-verbal, "Really?" Sensing his obvious reluctance, I followed it up with, "Just give it a try. See what happens."

The following week he came walking into class with excitement. "I have to admit," he said, "I was skeptical after our conversation last week, but I thought, I'm just going to do it to say I did it. I was sitting in my car in the college parking lot, still bothered by the B+. So I just asked out loud, 'Father, why is this test score bothering me so much? Why am I so mad about it?' Nothing, I heard nothing. I thought, 'Figures, I knew it was stupid to ask God.' So I started my car and drove off to get a pizza not giving the exercise another thought. By the time I got to the pizza place my mind had already moved on to several other things, but just as I opened the door to the pizza place, out of nowhere, a very vivid memory popped into my mind. It was an incredibly clear moment of when I was 10 years old. I was helping my dad work on the car. He asked me to hand him a wrench, but when I did, I accidently dropped it and it fell down into the engine of the car. I remember him just looking at me so frustrated saying, 'If you can't do something right, don't bother doing it at all!' There it was, an event that happened when I was 10, that I then associated with a lie and every time I wasn't 'perfect' the button to that lie was pushed. Not in a million years would I have connected that moment, which I had forgotten about, to the B+ I received on the quiz last week! I then asked, 'Father, what is your truth for that lie?' He gave me a scripture and it has forever changed me...it's amazing!"

So how do we go about changing an erroneous belief that is already in our heart?

- First, we must recognize the lie.

- Second, we must confront the lie and simply say, "That's not true."

- Third, we must replace the lie with the truth of God's Word and allow Father to speak His word to us.

When we are convinced in our heart of God's truth, our heart is healed at that moment. This takes place when accurate thoughts based on God's Word become a belief. Basing our beliefs on the Word of God will bring healing to our soul (mind, will and emotions).

Hebrews 4:12 (NIV) says, "For the word of God is alive and active. Sharper than any double-edged sword, it penetrates even to dividing soul and spirit, joints and marrow; it judges the thoughts and attitudes of the heart." The soul and spirit are so entwined there is only one thing that can separate the two and that is the Word of God.

We will address this subject in greater detail in a subsequent chapter. "Rhema" is a Greek word in the New Testament which is specifically defined as a "spoken word." The Holy Spirit will "speak" God's word to our hearts causing scripture to "jump off the page" giving us an "ah-ha" moment or a "light bulb moment" when His Word becomes extremely clear and personal to us. This "spoken word" will likely not be spoken in an audible sense, but God impresses His Word on our hearts in a unique way so that you know it is Him speaking to you through His Word.

In Revelation 1:16 (NIV) it says, "In his right hand he held seven stars, and out of his mouth came a sharp, double-edged sword. His face was like the sun shining in all its brilliance." It's very interesting that in this passage of Scripture which speaks of Jesus it says, "...out of his *mouth* came a sharp, double-edged sword." Typically how do you hold a sword? With your hand, of course. But that's not how Jesus holds the sword in this text. Jesus holds the sword with his mouth.

The first edge of the double-edged sword is God speaking it. The second edge is us declaring it. You need to hold the Word of God not in your hand but in your mouth. Holding the Bible in my hand does me no good. It brings life-changing power only when I put it through my eyes (reading), into my mind, and then ask God to speak His Word into my heart so I can declare it with my mouth. When I declare the Word of God, it becomes a mighty and powerful weapon. We need to hold the Sword the way Jesus holds the Sword in Revelation 1:16 and proclaim the Word of God.

Jesus said in John 8:32 (NIV), "Then you will know the truth, and the truth will set you free." We get the truth of God's word from our mind to our heart by meditating on the Word of God. We should want to read the Bible to be **in His presence**.

So many times when you talk to people they will say, "I know what the Bible says." Then they add, "...but, this is what I see in my life." We must get "I know what the Bible says" into a belief in our heart so what God's Word says is more real than what we experience in life. It must become the "source" of our truth.

Joshua 1:8 (NIV) says, "Keep this Book of the Law always on your lips; **meditate** on it day and night, so that you may be careful to do everything written in it. Then you will be prosperous and successful." Psalm 119:97 (NIV) says, "Oh, how I love your law! I **meditate** on it all day long." We need to meditate on the Word of God and memorize it.

You may or may not know that sheep are referred to as "ruminants." That means they have one stomach, but that stomach is divided into four sections. A sheep will take in the food it eats and after chewing and swallowing it goes into the first compartment. Then in a while the sheep will cough up the same food and will chew on it a little more before it goes into the second compartment. Then it comes back up and the sheep chews on it some more. This process happens over and over until the food finally reaches the fourth compartment of the stomach. Meditating on the Word of God is much the same way. We read it over and over and listen to what God is saying to us through those verses. We are digesting the Word of God. Isn't it interesting that Jesus said in John 10:27, "My sheep hear My voice, and I know them, and they follow Me."(NKJV)

Here is something that I found to be profound. You don't need to memorize the book of Romans or be a scholar of the

Greek language to be able to break The Cycle of a Stronghold and live an abundant Christian life. In Matthew 4 Jesus defeated the enemy by quoting three scriptures when he was tempted in the wilderness. Each time he said, "It is written" and went on to declare what was written. Game over! We need to meditate on the Word of God and memorize it so we can use it to defeat the enemy.

Have you ever had a song just pop into your head out of nowhere? I remember waking up one morning with a Bee Gee's song in my head. My first thought was, "What a great music era to have lived in. I loved listening to the Bee Gee's back in the day." Then I thought, "When was the last time I heard a Bee Gee's tune?" It had been a very, very long time ago. But it was in my memory somewhere from three decades ago and I woke up to that tune and was singing the song in the morning. It's amazing how long lasting our memories can be. Now, I have never even once woken up singing Snoop Dog's song, "Drop It Like It's Hot." Never, ever, has that happened. Do you know why? Because I never put that song in my mind. I was aware of the title, but I never listened to the song. I never memorized it. You don't remember things you don't memorize.

When you put yourself in the Word of God it gets into your mind then into your heart. Then, the moment a lie comes into your mind you will be able to use the Word of God to bring that thought into captivity. Jesus did it with three verses when he encountered the devil. In order for your soul to be healed, you must put yourself in the Word.

When you're in love with someone you don't have to be convinced to spend time with them. As you fall more in love with Jesus you will want to spend time in His Word. You will want to have it in your soul and spirit. You will want to meditate on it. You will want to use it to capture every thought. There are no shortcuts.

We want to read God's Word, not to learn about Him, but to sit and be with Him. And whenever we encounter a negative event, we sit with our Father and simply ask and listen: "Father, is there a lie I'm believing? What is the truth I should use to replace that lie?" I assure you, God's truth will <u>always</u> be found in His Word.

I encourage you right now to take a moment and be still before the Father. Then ask Him, "Father, is there a lie I am believing? If so, what is your truth?" Take the time necessary to hear what the Father is saying to you.

When we bring to God our brokenness and problems to fix, all we are bringing Him is our past. However, what God wants is our present and our future. God wants our hearts and our lives. We must bring to God not just our stumbling and failures, but also our heart.

In Galatians 2:20 (NIV) it says, "I have been crucified with Christ and I no longer live, but Christ lives in me. The life I now live in the body, I live by faith in the Son of God, who loved me and gave himself for me." If you have a struggle in your life, a stronghold, hurt or a wound, that is evidence there is still death residing in your soul. Your spirit is made new, but there is still death, pain and struggle that resides in your soul.

83

But as you come to Him with your heart and give Him those hurts and wounds, He takes the death, pain and struggle in your heart and replaces it with life.

That's what the story of the two trees was about. God desires that you eat of the Tree of Life and that you participate in the abundant life He sent His Son to purchase for you. Your belief system must come from the Word of God. "So then faith comes by hearing, and hearing by the word (rhema) of God" (Romans 10:17 NKJV).

Information will change your mind, but Revelation will change your heart, your beliefs and your life. When you understand the power of God's Word, then you will experience true life-giving changes in your beliefs and in our identity.

Take a few minutes right now and put into practice what I've been sharing in this chapter. Read and meditate on 2 Corinthians 5:17 (NKJV), "Therefore, if anyone *is* in Christ, *he is* a new creation; old things have passed away; behold, all things have become new."

Then ask, "Father, what does this Scripture mean for me?" Listen for God to respond. Write down what God tells you.

Next, read Philippians 4:13 (NKJV) – "I can do all things through Christ who strengthens me."

Ask: "Lord, is there anywhere in my life that my heart doesn't believe this? Again, listen for God to respond. Write down the areas of your life about which God speaks to you.

84

Finally, read Galatians 2:20 (NKJV) – "I have been crucified with Christ; it is no longer I who live, but Christ lives in me."

Ask: "Father, are there any areas of my life where I have not completely surrendered my life to you?" Listen for God to respond. Write down what God tells you.

When we bring God our brokenness and problems to fix, all we are bringing Him is our past; however, God also wants our present and our future.

Chapter 8

Fifth Level of Change – Identity Based Change

The Fifth Level of Change, Identity Based Change, is based on the premise that our identity can only come from our Heavenly Father. Romans 8:15-16 (NIV) gives us insight into our identity, "The Spirit you received does not make you slaves, so that you live in fear again; rather, the Spirit you received brought about your adoption to sonship. And by him we cry, "*Abba*, Father." [16] The Spirit himself testifies with our spirit that we are God's children."

Jesus also established the foundation for our identity when He said in John 15:5 (NIV), "I am the vine; you are the branches. If you remain in me and I in you, you will bear much fruit; apart from me you can do nothing."

Your identity can only be spoken by your Heavenly Father who created you. In fact Revelation 2:17 tells us that in the end, God will give us a white stone with our true name and identity on it. God wants you to know who you are in Christ. Part of the torture of those that don't give their life to Christ is the fact that they will never know their true name and identity.

Some time has now passed since the media build up, however, many of you will remember how the world watched via the tabloids and news as the former Olympian, Bruce Jenner, went through the process to transform himself into "Caitlyn." Now, in more recent reports, Jenner has indicated he may want to return to his original identity as "Bruce." This is just an example of the great lengths a wounded soul will go to in an attempt to find true identity.

In every person's heart is a desire to know who they are and only Jesus can answer that question. When we don't look to our Heavenly Father for the answer, we will take desperate measures seeking an answer. We are all driven to an extreme because that is how deep the passion for that question goes.

What we believe about God and what we believe about ourselves are vital elements because what we believe about ourselves, we transfer to God. If you believe you're worthless you will likely develop an erroneous logic that says, "I don't like myself, so God must be mad at me." It is inevitable that we will determine the value God places on us based on how we feel about ourselves. Even though God loves us unconditionally, we will only see His love through our own prism or perspective.

I personally went through a long-term struggle that illustrates this point quite well. As I was growing up I continuously struggled with an approval addiction and was always striving to be the best and always basing my identity on what I could accomplish. I eventually discovered that those tendencies we're connected to what became my nickname while growing up. As the last child born to my parents , I was dubbed the "oops baby."

This was also the beginning of "The Cycle of a Stronghold" which we discussed in the previous chapter. There was an event (an unplanned pregnancy) attached to a lie (I was an "oops" or a "mistake"). That resulted in a specific behavior in response to believing the lie. In my case, I had to be an achiever in order to feel valued. This behavior was then reinforced by others because they could likely see I felt valued when I was achieving.

I knew my parents loved me and I also knew God loved me and had a purpose for my life. But, in reality, these were just "thoughts" and not "beliefs." Deep down I was always striving to prove I wasn't an accident or an "oops baby." This "oops baby" belief carried on well into my adult years.

Then one morning during my quiet time with God, I was asking God to intervene regarding a situation at work. But all I was hearing from God was, "I knew you when I formed you in your mother's womb" (Jeremiah 1:5). I remember thinking, "Why can't I get this scripture out of my head?" Then I stopped and just listened to the words God was speaking. This verse from seemingly nowhere was actually God speaking to me. I don't remember when I had read that verse from Jeremiah 1:5, it realistically could have been months or possibly years earlier. But God was using those words as a "Rhema" word to me to affirm who I was; IT WAS NOW IN MY HEART. What I had as a "thought," suddenly became a "belief." When God changed my "belief" about being an "oops baby," and showed me that I was chosen, formed by

89

God and fearfully and wonderfully made, it changed my heart. Again, that truth went from a thought in my mind to a belief in my heart. When it became a belief in my heart, it was instantly a game changer. I was no longer bound by an approval addiction.

We all need to know we have worth and value. In fact, our search for our identity begins with this question, "what is my worth?" But we must understand while that question is important, it is much more important to pose that question to the right person.

If you are a baseball fan you have probably at least heard of some of the legendary players throughout the history of the sport. One of those names that became legendary in the very early years of the game was Honus Wagner, who was an outstanding shortstop for the Pittsburgh Pirates in the early 1900's. It was around this time that baseball cards of all the major league players were being produced. One of those cards featured the picture and statistics of the great Honus Wagner. In 1909 when the Honus Wagner card rolled off the presses it was likely produced for mere pennies. Little did anyone know at that time someone in the distant future, specifically 2007, would purchase that 1909 Honus Wagner baseball card for $2.8 million. You see, to the right person this card was worth millions.

Now the average person may not even pick up the card if it was lying on the ground. But to an expert...it's priceless! The difference is in who you ask.

If you ask the world what your worth is, you'll get a different answer. If you ask the world the worth of a fetus, many would say, "Well, it's not worth anything. You can just throw it away if you don't want it." But if you ask your Heavenly Father, he will say, "I knew you before I formed you in your mother's womb" (Jeremiah 1:5 NLT) and you are priceless. He will say, "You are fearfully and wonderfully made" (Psalm 139:14 NKJV) and "He who has begun a good work in you will complete it" (Philippians 1:6 NKJV).

You, my friend, are of great value in the eyes of God. He knew you before you were formed in your mother's womb. You have tremendous worth and you must not listen to anyone that would tell you otherwise! It is only God who can establish your true value and give you a genuine identity.

A number of years ago a Christian counselor friend of mine was driving to his office and saw a person walking down the street, but he couldn't tell if it was a man or a woman. The person looked like a woman, but her features were very masculine. Shortly after seeing this person walking he arrived at his office to meet with a new client for counseling. To his surprise, the person who entered his office for the counseling appointment was the same person he passed on the street. After meeting her face to face he realized that even up close it was difficult to identify the person's gender.

During the subsequent counseling sessions with her they began to peel back the many emotional layers of this young woman's life; all the sexual abuse and the hurts and wounds she was carrying. As he ministered to her over a period of time you could see healing come as the Word of God was ministered into her life.

Then, after a few counseling sessions he just called out the obvious. He said to her, "You know, God made you a woman." She looked at him and said, "Women are victims and weak and I will never be one." So he began to lay out the Scriptures and encouraged her to seek her identity through her Heavenly Father. A couple of weeks later he received a call from her at his office. She explained, "Pastor Bob, a strange thing just happened at work. I felt a little strange, so I went into the bathroom and I started my period." Pastor Bob responded with puzzlement, "Okay." She continued, "You don't understand, I'm 36 and I've never had a period." The lie she believed was so strong that it physically changed her as she grew up. The lie was so powerful that it caused her to lose her identity. But God's truth was so powerful that it allowed her to find her identity and become what she was created to be. **Her truth was no longer in her experience, but her source of truth became the Word of God and it was so powerful that it changed her thoughts, beliefs and even the organs in her body.**

Jesus said in John 8:32 (NIV), "Then you will know the truth, and the truth will set you free." Romans 10:17 (NKJV) tells us, "So then faith comes by hearing, and hearing by the word (rhema) of God." When God gives a word of revelation (a rhema word), things change because His word has creative power. The sound of His voice literally creates things. You will find evidence of this in the very first chapter of the Bible. God literally "spoke," everything that was created.

Remember, it's not the question, but who you ask that's important. Seek Him with all of your heart; and when you seek Him you will find Him. Seek Him about your identity, value and worth. Walk in the promise of sonship and the promise of daughtership. Rather than focus on your strongholds and your hurts or your behavior, focus on what God is telling you about your identity and how He sees you.

As I mentioned earlier, when we bring to God our brokenness and problems to fix, all we are bringing Him is our past. However, God also wants our *present* and our *future*. God wants our hearts and our lives. We must bring to God not just our stumbling and failures, but also our heart.

Galatians 2:20 (NIV) says, "I have been crucified with Christ and I no longer live, but Christ lives in me. The life I now live in the body, I live by faith in the Son of God, who loved me and gave himself for me." This tells me that if you have a struggle in your life, a stronghold, hurt or a wound, it is evidence there is still *death* residing in your soul. If you have accepted Jesus as your personal Savior, there is no doubt your spirit has been made new and is full of life from God, but there is still death that resides in your soul (mind, will and emotions).

As we come to God with our hearts and give Him those hurts and wounds, He takes the death in our hearts and replaces it with life. That's what the story of the two trees was about. God desires that you eat of the Tree of Life and that you participate in the abundant life He sent His son to purchase for you.

Your belief system must come from the Word of God. When you begin to see what is in the Father's heart when He sees you, you will begin to experience healing and freedom. Psalm 139:14 (NIV) declares, "I praise you because <u>I am fearfully and wonderfully made</u>; your works are wonderful, I know that full well."

The reality is that "behavior" is simply the fruit of the problem. The real issue is in your identity. You don't have a pornography issue, you have an identity issue. You don't have a relationship issue, you have an identity issue. You don't have a marriage crisis, you have an identity issue.

When you recognize the the identity the Father has given you, it will immediately change your beliefs, your source of truth, your willpower and your behavior. Then, and only then, you will find peace in any environment. In fact, you will have peace in spite of your environment.

When the Apostle Paul was in prison he wrote a great portion of the Bible referred to as the "Prison Epistles" which are Ephesians, Philippians, Colossians and Philemon. Even while in a physical prison Paul was living his purpose and living in freedom as he was encouraging and freeing others through his writing.

I encourage you to take a moment right now to apply these truths to your life. 1 John 4:4 **(NIV) says,** "You, dear children, are from God and have overcome them, because the One who is in you is greater than the one who is in the world."

Take some time to meditate on 1 John 4:4 above. Then pray, "Father, I want to believe and hold this truth in my heart. Speak and confirm this to me." Take a few moments to be silent before Father and listen to Him, allowing Him to confirm this to your heart.

2 Corinthians 5:17 (NKJV) declares, "Therefore, if anyone *is* in Christ, *he is* a new creation; old things have passed away; behold, all things have become new." After meditating on this Scripture, ask God this question, "Father, what does this Scripture mean for me?" Then listen for God to respond. Write down what God speaks to you.

Forgiveness is a choice, not an emotion.

Chapter 9

Forgiveness

When the enemy loses the battle for your spirit, he then shifts his tactics to your mind, will and emotions to keep you captive and keep you convinced that the jail cell is still locked. He wants you to be convinced that there is no hope for you or that you will be just fine if you can simply cope with life as you know it. However, as we have already established, God desires for you to live an abundant life. He wants you to live in victory, not succumb to the schemes and divisiveness of the enemy.

In my ministry I have come to the conclusion that the two most common barriers that keep people from discovering healing, power and restoration in their lives are *pride* and *unforgiveness*. This is a very important chapter because you will not find freedom and healing until you learn to forgive. If there are only two things you take away from this book, it should be:

1. **You must learn to forgive if you want to be healed and set free - No Exceptions.**

2. Your Heavenly Father will give you the strength to forgive, because He wants you healed and set free.

Unforgiveness can be a difficult lesson to learn, but the bible shows us the path to healing. Most people have a general understanding that as Christians we are to forgive. But we must understand and learn how to forgive from our heart.

Forgiveness is a requirement for all believers because it is so powerful in bringing freedom into our lives. Matthew 18:23-35 (NKJV) tells us that a person, even though they are a Christian, can be tormented in their life if they aren't willing to forgive:

[23] Therefore the kingdom of heaven is like a certain king who wanted to settle accounts with his servants. [24] And when he had begun to settle accounts, one was brought to him who owed him ten thousand talents. [25] But as he was not able to pay, his master commanded that he be sold, with his wife and children and all that he had, and that payment be made. [26] The servant therefore fell down before him, saying, 'Master, have patience with me, and I will pay you all.' [27] Then the master of that servant was moved with compassion, released him, and forgave him the debt. [28] "But that servant went out and found one of his fellow servants who owed him a hundred denarii; and he laid hands on him and took *him* by the throat, saying, 'Pay me what you owe!' [29] So his fellow servant fell down at his feet and begged him, saying, 'Have patience with me, and I will pay you all.' [30] And he would not, but went and threw him into prison till he should pay the debt. [31] So when his fellow servants saw what had been done, they were very grieved, and came and told

their master all that had been done. [32] Then his master, after he had called him, said to him, 'You wicked servant! I forgave you all that debt because you begged me. [33] Should you not also have had compassion on your fellow servant, just as I had pity on you?' [34] And his master was angry, and delivered him to the torturers until he should pay all that was due to him. "So My heavenly Father also will do to you if each of you, from his heart, does not forgive his brother his trespasses."

It's important to note that it is not God torturing us, He is a loving God. But when we won't forgive, our unwillingness to trust Him and obey leaves a door open in our life for the enemy to enter. It's for this reason that Father God is asking us to trust Him, to cast our cares upon Him, receive His forgiveness daily for our own life and then extend that forgiveness to others. In doing so, it closes the door to the tormentor in our life. Jesus tells us in Matthew 10:8, "Freely you have received, freely you must give" (NIV).

The torture that comes as a result of unforgiveness can manifest in many ways. It can develop into depression, anxiety, a state of hopelessness, a series of failed relationships, addictions, even physical ailments. **Unforgiveness leads to bondage in our life.**

The effects of unforgiveness can be far reaching. The above passage in Matthew 18 indicates unforgiveness can turn into "wickedness" in our hearts. The servant in this parable was no doubt defensive when his master called him "wicked." He may have said something like, "What do you mean calling me wicked? He owed me money. I'm the victim here. He's the

99

wicked one for not paying me back." How many times do we see ourselves as the victim and feel we are the one that has been wronged and the other person is the wicked one?

When we hold on to unforgiveness it gives the enemy a door into our life. That is, it gives the enemy permission to come into our life. In this story Jesus indicates the servant was "handed over to the jailers" or "torturers." When we don't forgive, we place ourselves in a spiritual jail and bondage as we then begin to carry bitterness. It has been said, holding on to unforgiveness to get back at someone is like drinking poison and waiting for the other person to die.

For our deepest hurts, it may be impossible to forgive relying upon our own strength and ability. But with the power and grace found in Christ we can learn to forgive all others all the time. Yes, we can actually live a life of forgiveness. The power of the cross brings freedom to those who are willing to call upon Christ's strength to forgive. Philippians 4:13 (NKJV) encourages us by letting us know this truth, "I can do all things through Christ who strengthens me." It is possible for us to forgive the way we are called to forgive with the power of God in our life.

In Psalm 55:12-14 (NIV) David is lamenting when he writes this: "If an enemy were insulting me, I could endure it. If a foe was rising against me, I could hide. But it is you, a man like myself, my companion, my close friend, with whom I once enjoyed sweet fellowship at the house of God, as we walked among the worshippers." The people who are closest to us have the greatest ability to hurt us. These are often the most difficult cases of forgiveness. So, how do we walk through that hurt and come to a place of forgiveness toward a close friend or relative that has hurt us deeply?

David said, "If you were a stranger or an enemy, I could deal with it. But you were a friend; you were a brother." Sometimes, when the pain is so deep, we don't know what to do with the hurt and the wound.

We must ultimately follow the teaching of Jesus on this subject. Jesus said very plainly in Luke 17:3-4 (NIV), "If your brother sins, rebuke him, and if he repents, forgive him. If he sins against you seven times in a day, and seven times comes back to you and says, 'I repent,' forgive him."

I love the disciples' response: "Are you kidding me? If a brother sins against me seven times in a day, I need to forgive him, really? We can't do it. You need to increase our faith" (paraphrasing Luke 7:5).

This is where Jesus said, "If you have faith as small as a mustard seed, you can say to this mulberry tree, 'Be uprooted and planted in the sea,' and it will obey you" (Luke 17:6 NIV). The mustard seed is the tiniest of all seeds that grows the biggest tree in proportion to its size. What Jesus is saying is that all you must have is the desire to forgive and he will do the rest. Let's examine the steps to being able to really forgive as Jesus instructs.

Steps to Forgiveness

Step 1: You Must have the Desire to Walk in Forgiveness.

This subject is very relevant because this issue touches everyone. You may say, "Well, I just don't get offended." But, that's impossible. Luke 17:1 (NKJV) tells us this: "It is impossible that no offenses should come, but woe to him through whom they do come." What Jesus is saying in this passage is simply that there is no way you're going to go through life without being offended. Being offended sometime is just part of life. The reality is that very possibly right now you are in a state of being offended or there will be a time in the near future when you will be offended. You can't ignore it or sweep it under the rug. It's going to happen.

This was a message Jesus was so passionate about that he proclaimed it and taught it with the very last breath of his life. Luke 23:34 (NKJV): "Then Jesus said, 'Father, forgive them, for they do not know what they do.' And they divided His garments and cast lots." Sometimes we forget that while Jesus was the Son of God, he walked as a man during his ministry on earth. Everything he did on earth he did as a man, looking to the Father for strength, so we can do it as well.

Jesus was the prime example of one who exhibited forgiveness. He was whipped 39 times, according to culture, with a "cat o' nine tails." A cat o' nine tails was a whip with nine different frays on it with chards of bone or metal on the tips of each fray. The personnel inflicting this punishment stopped beating him after 39 lashes because most would die at 40 and they wanted to keep Jesus alive. After 39 times of being hit with this whip you could see organs inside the body cavity.

He then hung on a cross which was death by suffocation because the prisoner's lungs would eventually start to collapse. Nails were driven through the victim's legs and when he would try to push himself up to catch his breath from the failing lung function, there would be excruciating pain. The victim would inhale, then collapse again due to the pain and return to suffocation.

There was a thief on one side of him that shouted derogatory statements toward him and a thief on the other side that recognized who Jesus was and asked for forgiveness. Jesus responded through his agonizing pain, "Today you will be with me in paradise" (Luke 23:43 NKJV).

People on the ground grumbled, "He can save others, but can't save himself." Then, with one of his last breaths he uttered, "Father, forgive them for they know not what they do" (Luke 23:34 KJV).

Jesus died as a "forgiver." He was not going to die a captive, but he would die as one who sets people free. If Jesus would have died with unforgiveness in his heart, he would have been captive to unforgiveness.

Jesus declares to us that with the same power he was able to forgive, we too can forgive others. It is very important to see that in Jesus' last breath on earth he is demonstrating to us that we must forgive others if we want to be set free.

Unforgiveness is a lie the enemy uses as he seeks to destroy us. One of the lies we believe is that we can hold on to unforgiveness and contain it in our lives. We think, "I can be angry at my boss or co-worker and not have it affect my wife and kids." We persuade ourselves to think we can target and isolate bitterness in one area of our lives but not have it affect other areas of our lives. But the stark reality is that you can't isolate unforgiveness to just one individual.

2 Timothy 2:26 (NIV) says, "…that they would come to their senses and escape the snare of the devil, having been taken captive by him to do his will." Without question, unforgiveness is a "snare of the devil." If you have ever seen a coyote snare or trap, you know that trap may just hold on to the animal's paw, but it has in essence captured its whole body. It may hold only one small part of his body, but by so doing it actually has captured the entire body. So it is with unforgiveness.

For some, the hurt is so bad, you can't imagine "just forgiving" someone; you wouldn't even know where to begin and if you were being honest, the pain and hurt is so bad, you don't even have a desire to forgive. Sexual abuse is one of the most devastating betrayals to face. One in three people are sexually abused. Another deep wound that we see in society is divorce. As we read in the scripture by David, it's the people closest to us that have the ability to hurt us the most.

104

I personally went through a horrific time of hurt and betrayal. While it was devastating, through the experience I learned to trust my Heavenly Father as He revealed the path to forgiveness, healing and freedom.

During my high school years I dated a girl who I eventually married shortly after graduation. We had been married for just eleven months when I discovered she had been having an affair for the past two months. Nothing rips your heart out like the betrayal of adultery and divorce. We were very young; I was only 21 at the time. I told her I wasn't going to fight her for any material things. I said, "Just come and take what you're going to take." She definitely took advantage of that opportunity and took me up on my offer. One day her dad and boyfriend came over with a truck and her boyfriend grabbed one end of my couch and I grabbed the other end and we loaded my couch in his truck. I watched everything go out the door that day.

Every so often I would see him driving around town in my car. There was one particular time I had to deal with this subject of unforgiveness. It was about one o'clock in the morning and I was lying in bed when my answering machine went off. Yes, prior to voicemail there were these antique machines we called "answering machines." On those machines you could hear the person's voice as they left their message. It was my ex-wife calling. She said, "I'm leaving an envelope in my parents' mailbox. If it's still there in the morning, I'm taking it out. If you want to read what's in it, come and get it tonight." At that point I was still hoping for reconciliation and I thought maybe this was a letter that would lead to reconciliation or at least an apology. Then I thought, maybe it's a trap. As I lay there it was driving me crazy so I decided to get up and go get the letter out of the mailbox. Around 3 a.m. I drove across town to her parents' house. I opened the mailbox and found a blue envelope and the contents felt like there were several pages. The envelope was sealed. So I drove home with a sense of excitement and anticipation.

When I opened the envelope I found four pages with writing on both sides of each page. The letter started off by saying, "I can't believe how stupid you were." She continued, "All those times when you answered the phone and the caller hung up, that was my boyfriend calling. We used to laugh because you weren't catching on." She also said, "The necklace I always wore that you would always comment on was a gift from my boyfriend on Valentine's Day and I would laugh whenever you commented on it because I knew where it came from. I would wear it in front of you knowing the secret behind it and what we were doing." This type of thing went on for four double-sided handwritten pages. For the next two days there was so much anger inside me I thought, "If I see this man I'm going to kill him." I even began thinking, "How can I kill him and get away with it?" I wasn't planning on it, but I was thinking about how I could do it and not get caught. The rage and the hurt were so strong that I didn't want to forgive. I felt that if I forgave, it was going to let them off the hook and I wanted them to hurt just like they hurt me.

I have discovered that there are two different kinds of people that walk in hurts, offenses and wounds: those who were truly mistreated and those that simply think they were a victim. But the Bible shows no distinction between the two. **It doesn't matter how legitimate your offense is, He calls you to forgive.** Why? Because He wants you to be set free and bitterness will keep you captive.

Step 2: Forgive Yourself.

The reason people can't forgive is because they have not fully received the forgiveness Jesus offered them. If you're walking with shame and guilt and condemnation, it is because you have not embraced the fact that you are fully forgiven. You have not fully embraced that on the cross Jesus pushed himself up one more time to inhale just so He could say, "Forgive them."

In Psalm 103:2-4 (NIV) it says, "Praise the Lord, my soul, and forget not all his benefits - who forgives all your sins and heals all your diseases, who redeems your life from the pit and crowns you with love and compassion." **In Matthew 10:8 (NIV), Jesus said, "Freely you have received, freely give." You cannot give what you don't have. You have to receive His forgiveness for yourself before you can give it to others.** In Galatians 3:14 (NIV) it says, "…He redeemed us." Accept the forgiveness God has already provided for you, then you will be positioned to forgive others.

In Matthew 6:9-12 (KJV), when Jesus teaches the disciples how to pray, He said to pray in this manner, "Our Father which art in heaven, hallowed be thy name. Thy kingdom come. Thy will be done on earth, as it is in heaven. Give us this day our daily bread. <u>And forgive us our debts</u> (sins), as <u>we forgive our</u>

debtors (or those that have sinned against us)." We have to receive forgiveness before we can extend forgiveness.

To get out of the bitterness and anger you may be experiencing, begin giving thanks that you are forgiven. Every day in your quiet time just simply say, "Lord, thank you that you have forgiven me; I receive your full forgiveness today." As you declare this day after day during your quiet time your heart will start to receive it and believe that you are truly forgiven.

Step 3: Pray for Your Offender.

In John 15:5 (NIV) Jesus says, "Apart from me you can do nothing." Matthew 5:44 (NIV) instructs us in this way, "Love your enemies and pray for those that persecute you." You may not be able to "love your enemies" at first, but when you begin to receive God's forgiveness in your own life, it will give you His strength and healing which will enable you to forgive others.

Simply make this your prayer, "Lord, thank you for forgiving me and I choose to forgive others." Forgiveness is a choice, not an emotion. The emotion will eventually follow your choice. When your tongue confesses it, it is like the rudder of a ship and your emotions will follow your confession.

Step 4: Pray Blessings Over Your Offender.

In the illustration given above about the betrayal of my spouse, the Holy Spirit quickened something in my spirit. The Holy Spirit said, "I want you to start praying blessings over them." I

108

said, "I don't want to do that because then you'll bless them and then I'll be mad at you." Initially, I didn't want them blessed. In fact, I really wanted God to smite them and have His wrath come down upon them. I wanted every plague, sickness and disease to be upon their home. I wanted every flat tire and broken transmission to visit them. I wanted to be able to laugh at them and say, "It serves you right!"

It took everything I had to forgive them, but to pray blessing on them, I just didn't want to do it. But the Holy Spirit said, "Do you want me to bless you? If you want me to bless you, then you need to pray blessings on them." You see, the Holy Spirit was trying to bring me to a place of healing.

In Luke 6:27-28 (NIV) Jesus said, "But I tell you who hear me, love your enemies, do good to those who hate you, bless those who curse you, pray for those who mistreat you." So I finally said, "Lord, thank you for forgiving me. I choose to forgive them." Then I finally said curtly, "and Lord, bless them." At that moment the Holy Spirit spoke to me and said, "I want you to pray blessings on them the same way you want me to bless you." I thought, "Are you kidding me?" I then recalled what my dad would say when I was a child, "James, go mow the lawn." I would reply, "Oh, okay." Then he would say, "And do it with a good attitude!" It wasn't enough that I mowed the lawn; I had to do it with a good attitude.

My Heavenly Father was saying to me, "You pray blessings on them and you do it with a good attitude. You pray for them the way you want me to respond in your life." To this day I distinctly remember that moment of freedom; that moment of declaration when I finally got to that point.

109

I was faithful to receive God's forgiveness, I was faithful to forgive them, and on that day I was able to genuinely say, "Lord, bless them." It took a while, but I was eventually able to get to the point of praying blessings over them. When I said those words, "Lord, bless them," I then had compassion and understood why that letter was written. It was because there were many hurts and wounds in their lives. We do stupid things when we're hurt and we're wounded. It was then that I realized hurting people hurt people and they were no different than I was. It was then that I found healing and prayed they would discover God the way I had discovered Him. I prayed for healing, restoration, and favor over their lives (which are God's blessings). As I began to declare those things it gave me energy as I was receiving the things I was declaring through faith in Jesus Christ. In that moment when I was declaring all that greatness over them, I began to receive it into my own life.

It has been years later and my life has been fully restored and healed. I have been blessed beyond my imagination. I could run into that couple today and it would not bother me in the least. That is what healing and freedom looks like and it's only possible through the power of Jesus Christ.

Before concluding this subject of forgiveness, it's important to say that you can forgive people and still keep healthy boundaries. I want to be clear. Forgiveness doesn't mean full access to a relationship that would allow someone hurt or abuse again. One can forgive someone and still establish new healthy boundaries. In 1 Samuel 24:8-10 David honored and forgave Saul for wanting to kill him, but he did so from a distance. You have the ability and right to forgive from a distance those that seek to harm you.

Take a moment to meditate on this promise of God in 1 John 4:4 (NKJV): "You are of God, little children, and have overcome them, because He who is in you is greater than he who is in the world."

Pray, "Father, thank you for the forgiveness you have given. I receive your forgiveness in my life. I declare, in Jesus's name, that I am forgiven. As I freely receive, I freely give. I choose to forgive all others. I choose to forgive specifically _____ in Jesus's name."

Write in the line above the name or names of individuals you will forgive. Even though it may seem difficult, remember, "He who is in you is greater than he who is in the world." You can do this!

God desires to have a powerful, life-giving relationship with us.

Chapter 10

Hearing God

The first step to hearing God is to understand that God's Word, the Bible, is supernatural, full of power, and overflowing with abundant life. The actual words written on the pages of your personal Bible are literally life-giving. We find in Scripture that God's breath contains life and God's words create.

Whatever God breathes on comes to life. Genesis 2:7 (KJV) records the account of the creation of man, "And the Lord God formed man of the dust of the ground, and <u>breathed</u> into his nostrils <u>the breath of life</u>; and man became a living soul." The life-giving breath of God is also evidenced in the New Testament where the Apostle Paul says in 2 Timothy 3:16 (NKJV), "All scripture is <u>God-breathed</u> and is useful for teaching, rebuking, correcting and training in righteousness. Just as He did with Adam, God did with His Word. So, as we read the Bible to *listen* and not just read to learn, the Bible brings life to us and healing to our soul.

Not only does God's breath bring life, but God's words create. God can't say something without creating it. In Genesis 1:3 (KJV) God created through His words, "And God said, 'Let there be light' and there was light." In Mark 4:39 Jesus spoke and rebuked the wind and said to the sea, "Peace, be still!" The wind immediately ceased and the waves were simultaneously calmed. He spoke "peace" and peace was created.

We also see in Scripture that God's Word can be received in two different forms. This is identified by two Greek words that are both translated "word" in the English language, but each have a more specific meaning. The first Greek word is "Logos." This is the *written* word that is studied, taught and memorized.

The second word is "Rhema" which means to *utter* or *say*. It is God *speaking* His word to you. Romans 10:17 (NKJV) uses the word "Rhema," "So then faith comes by hearing, and hearing by the *word* of God." In other words, "Faith comes from hearing God speak to us through His Word."

Hebrews 11:6 (NKJV) tells us, "But without faith it is impossible to please Him, for he who comes to God must believe that He is, and that He is a rewarder of those who diligently seek Him." We can't please God without faith and we can't develop faith without hearing His voice or His "Rhema" Word. When we put these scriptures together, it is telling us what pleases God the most isn't us trying harder. It's when you and I, His children, come to Him seeking to hear His voice; to talk with Him; to be with Him; to diligently seek Him. These things please God. And, we can only do that through faith that comes from hearing a "Rhema" Word from God. Just like God's original relationship with Adam and Eve in the garden, He desires to have a powerful, life-giving relationship with us.

Both "Logos" and "Rhema" are vital to our relationship with God. In fact, God will use "Logos" to give us a "Rhema." An amazing example of how God uses His "Logos" and "Rhema" word to bring the supernatural into the natural was seen in one of the most traumatizing ministry encounters I have ever faced. A very dear couple who were extremely faithful to the church asked to meet with me between services. When I shut the door, they both began to sob. "What's going on?" I asked. Through the tears I learned the husband had just been to a doctor's appointment the day before where he was told they discovered cancer. He showed no symptoms and felt great. It was during routine blood work that it was discovered. But the news was going to get worse. The doctor said, "It can't be treated. It's very aggressive and you only have four weeks to live." "WHAT!? You look perfectly healthy." I exclaimed.

We all cried and I said, "I'm going to bring another pastor in and we are going to pray for you, but you need to seek God for a word! You need to hear Him speak His written word to you. You need to hear a Rhema word."

After that meeting he went back for a second visit and they said the cancer was moving even more aggressively than they had thought and that he needed to get his affairs in order very soon. Later that week, he couldn't sleep so he got up in the middle of the night to read his Bible. His daily reading was Mark 4:39 where Jesus rebuked the wind and said to the sea, "Peace, be still!" He remembered saying, "Father, I need your peace," and went back to bed. Later that morning, on his way to work, he was listening to a preacher on the radio. Guess what the pastor was preaching on? You probably guessed it- Mark 4:39. He

115

said to himself, "Hey, that's the passage I read in the middle of the night. That's amazing." Then when he arrived at work and pulled into his parking spot, there on the car in front of him was a bumper sticker that read, "Mark 4:39 - Know His Peace." When he read it out aloud, he felt the peace and presence of God. He said, "I knew I was healed in that moment."

With his next doctor visit the following day, he insisted a new test be taken. In a resolute manner he said to the doctor, "I am healed; I know I am healed!" The doctors were reluctant, and said, "Because there is no reason to believe things have changed, the insurance probably won't cover the cost of the test." He responded, "I don't care, I'll pay for it. We need to do another scan. I know I'm healed!" Upon his insistence, a new scan was ordered and the cancer was completely gone. The doctors said they have never seen this type of cancer "go away". That was three years ago and he continues to serve God and enjoy life.

God speaks to each of us on a **personal level** and when we hear His voice, it 1.) contains His breath which brings life and 2.) The sound of His voice creates what He is telling us (i.e. PEACE!). God speaks on a macro level to mankind through the "Logos" Word of God. He also speaks on a micro level to each person who will listen a 'Rhema" Word. John 10:27 (NKJV) Jesus said, "My sheep hear My voice, and I know them, and they follow Me."

In fact, in order for us to live an abundant life as a Christian it is foundational that we learn to hear the voice of God. God wants to speak and He will speak to you. For some, today God is about to speak to you for the first time. By hearing God speak to us and accepting what he is saying, we will change our way of thinking.

Whenever the subject of "Hearing God" comes up, there are typically many questions that surround recognizing God's voice. How do we recognize the voice of God? How do we know what God sounds like? How do we know what He is trying to say?

Many people find it difficult to hear God speak to them because they are more focused on trying to live their perception of a Christian life than they are trying to hear God speak to them. Living a life of freedom that God intends for you isn't about trying harder, but it's about hearing the voice of God. We seem to have the mentality that if we just try harder not to do something or if we try harder to be better, then we can walk in freedom. But freedom comes from hearing the Spirit of God speak into our hearts.

The Apostle Paul said in 2 Corinthians 3:17 (NIV), "Where the Spirit of the Lord is, there is freedom." In order to experience that freedom, it is so important that we dial in to hear what the Spirit of the Lord is saying. Our effort shouldn't be in trying to get God to answer, but for us to be quiet enough to listen.

What would you say if I were to ask you, "Where is the nearest radio station located?" You would likely tell me the physical location of the station and you could even look up the physical address. You could then put the address into a GPS that will give you very specific directions to the radio station. But couldn't you also scientifically say that the radio station is right there in the room you are in right now? Even if you're outside, you could say the station is right there. It's all around you. It's under your feet. It's above your head. It's in the air. Yet, you can't hear it and you can't touch it. But, if you had a receiver such as a radio, you could plug it in, turn on the power, tune it to the station, and you could hear everything being broadcast. In fact, you would likely find out there are probably dozens of radio stations right now in the air to which you could listen if you tuned into their frequency. All you need is power and a tuner and you would be able to enjoy the music or information that is being dispersed through the air waves on that station.

Hearing God is much like that. The power source is Jesus Christ and the receiver is the Holy Spirit that He put within you. When we plug into the power – when we receive Jesus Christ – and we allow the Holy Spirit to tune our hearts, we begin to see that the Kingdom of God is at hand and the power of God is at hand.

Psalm 46:10 (NKJV) tells us to, "Be still and know that I am God." Jeremiah 29:13 (NASB) says, "You will seek Me and find Me when you search for Me with all your heart." Matthew 7:7 (NASB) tells us, "Ask and it will be given to you; seek and you will find; knock and the door will be opened to you." Again, faith isn't dependent upon us trying harder; faith is about us hearing God speak into our hearts. Our faith is built when God breathes His Word into our heart and gives it life and when He speaks His Word into our life and creates His will for us to enjoy.

To hear God speak we must also understand how we are made. Psalm 139:14 (NKJV) tells us we are "fearfully and wonderfully made." Each of us are unique and God seems to speak to us, for the most part, according to the way we learn. Educators and psychologists say there are basically three ways that we learn.

Vision Focused Learners

For these types of learners, there might be a time when you're worshipping and you close your eyes and all of a sudden you have this image or picture in your mind. Some people simply are very visual and God will give them an image or possibly a dream.

Audible Learners

Audible learners can hear God speak to their heart. He speaks clearly through words that they hear in their heart. It's not unusual for a pastor to have someone come to them after a sermon and say, "Pastor, that's exactly what I needed to hear." The reason that happens is not because the pastor is that good and it's not because he hacked into their email. It is simply because your pastor believes with all his heart that if he sits quietly before God He will speak to his heart the word that is needed for individuals who will be in attendance. Your pastor goes before God every week and asks, "Lord, what do you want me to share with the church?" God knows the things you are seeking. He knows the things that you're struggling with and He will download those things to your pastor as he prepares to speak to the congregation week after week. And that results in you walking out of a service saying, "That's exactly what I needed." It is the power of God speaking into our lives.

One time during a mid-week service I was sitting in my usual seat during worship. The worship team was just melting the place down. I remember thinking, "This is amazing!" Then I glanced over the church and all of a sudden God began reminding me of testimonies and the stories of the people sitting in that room. And every time I looked at someone he said to me, "Remember their story; remember when you prayed with them when they were dealing with this and I did that in their life?" Then I looked at someone else and He said, "Remember when they gave their life to Christ?" And I looked at someone else and He said, "Remember their story?" I was hearing all these things of what God has done over the years and it was just a powerful moment to be able to share. God often speaks to my heart in that way. That's the way I hear.

Hands On Learners (or those that "Learn by Doing")

Many times I have talked to hunters – deer hunters especially – and they tell me when they're out in their deer blind and the sun is coming up and in that experience of doing something, God reveals Himself to them and they experience the peace of God. A lot of people that ride motorcycles say that is when God speaks to them. They have conveyed, when they are out riding it's not unusual for the peace of God to envelope them. For these types of learners, it's when they are doing something that they experience a connection with God.

120

Once you become aware of how God created you to understand how He will connect with you, it will help you to know how to tune in to what God is saying. But know this, no matter what type of learner you may be, God is desperate to speak to His children. Hearing God should not be weird or make you feel uncomfortable. There may have been times when you heard someone say, "God told me...," and you respond with, "Oh boy, here we go." I don't want you to think hearing from God is weird, but at the same time, we must also know that God sometimes does some pretty unusual things to speak to us. But usually, He speaks to us when we are still before Him and we are not distracted by other things.

It is the nature of God to want to talk to His children. If you look at the Old Testament you'll find some crazy and weird ways He chose to talk to people. Not only does He talk to us through His Word or the Law in the Old Testament, but there was one time in the book of Daniel where His hand (a big giant hand) was seen writing on the wall. Now that would be a bit freaky. In the book of Numbers, God spoke through Balaam's donkey. God has done some crazy things because He is passionate about getting this message across, "I am your God and you are my people."

When He speaks to us at the heart level, it changes things. Knowledge tells us how to think, but revelation tells us how to believe. God wants to speak revelation to our hearts. He wants to replace the lies that the world has put in our heart that say we're not good enough and that we should live with shame and guilt. Rather than deal with us just on a knowledge level, He wants to speak to what we believe. He will speak directly to

121

our hearts and replace those lies with the truth about how He sees us and who He is.

In our one o'clock service we have about a dozen people from the deaf community that attend and we have an interpreter that signs for them. One of the deaf folks came to me after the service and said through the interpreter, "Pastor, I'm not sure if this is God or not but I was watching the movie, 'Taken,' and I felt the Holy Spirit speak to my heart when I saw the dad in the movie go to any length to rescue his daughter and He said, 'I do the same for you. I will go to any lengths to rescue you.' And I began to cry." Then she asked, "Was that God?" I said, "Because the basic truth is found in the Bible, it has all the indications that what you heard was God speaking to you in that moment."

Yes, I believe God can reveal truths to us on a very personal level even through a secular movie. God wants to speak to you and it will change your life. It will enable your natural to connect to His supernatural when you hear His voice.

To hear God speak, not only must we understand how we are made, but we must also be still. I will be the first to admit that to learn how to be quiet and still before the Lord is a learned skill. It doesn't necessarily come easy in today's culture that is busy, busy, busy. But we must **learn** to be quiet and be still. Psalm 46:10 (NIV) says, "Be still and know that I am God." The only way you will learn that He is God is to be still before Him.

Isaiah 40:31 (NKJV) says, "But those who **wait on the LORD** shall renew *their* strength; They shall mount up with wings like eagles, they shall run and not be weary, they shall walk and not faint." It's when we learn to **wait upon Him** and to rest in Him and to be quiet before Him that we receive strength and then we will become connected to His power.

In 1 Kings 19:11-12 the prophet Elijah didn't hear God in the loud wind, earthquake or fire, but in a "still, small voice." God doesn't always speak to us in real demonstrative ways. In fact, most often He speaks to us in very subtle, but distinct ways. We have to learn how He created us; then we have to learn to be still and to listen.

The good thing is that we don't have to be in the dark about what God wants to say to us because He speaks to us through the Word of God. When God speaks a specific word to us, it will always, without exception, be in perfect harmony with the written Word. If you can believe it, I've actually had someone say to me, "Pastor, God told me to divorce my wife and marry this woman" – and they were serious. That message was not confirmed anywhere in the Word of God. When God speaks to us it *always* will affirm what is already written.

You will have a hard time hearing God if you're not reading the Word of God. In John 1:1 (NIV) it says, "In the beginning was the Word, and the Word was with God, and the Word was God." God *lives and breathes* within the Scriptures.

Apparently my voice is loud and distinct because I've been told more than one time in a very polite way that I don't have an "indoor voice." I've had people come up to me and say, "You were at the movie Friday night, weren't you?" I said, "Yes, actually I was. How did you know?" They responded, "We could hear you laugh." In a theatre full of people evidently my laugh is very specific and identifiable. When we are at a restaurant, my wife tells me I need to whisper and I tell her "I am whispering." She will say, "No you're not; the people on the other side are listening to our conversation. You have to use an indoor voice." She also tells me, "When we're at church and I can't find you, all I have to do is listen and I can locate you." She can hear my voice in a room of hundreds of people apparently because it's a little louder than everyone else. She knows my voice because she knows me and she's with me every day. Next to Christ, we are the closest in relationship and in a crowd of people my voice is very specific to her ear and she can hear my voice over all the other voices competing in the room.

It's the same way that a mom in a nursery with 20 kids knows the cry of her child as opposed to the cries of other children. Why is that? It's because there is an intimacy, bond and connection that makes that voice or that cry specific and it resonates within a mom's heart.

In much the same way, we learn to hear the voice of God through the Word of God. As we become familiar with the "voice of God" through His Word, we learn to hear His distinct voice. Sometimes the words jump off the page and at other times there may be weeks or months that go by and God speaks to us through a Scripture we read weeks or months before. Psalm 119:105 (NKJV) says, "Your word is a lamp to my feet and a light to my path." The Word of God will literally direct your path, your calling, your will and your purpose for your life. If you're a student, if you're just going into a relationship, or if you have grandkids on the way; wherever you're at in life, the Word of God lights our path and it will lead and guide us because the voice of God resides in it and it speaks to our hearts.

God also speaks through prophetic word. That means He chooses someone else to speak His truth to us. A friend of mine was at a pretty big conference with a lot of people in attendance and right in the middle of a lecture the speaker stopped, looked right at the person sitting next to my friend, and said, "God wants to call you Jeffery." My friend looked at him and saw he was wearing a name badge with the name "Jeff" on it and thought, "Okay, there's no big stretch there." Then the speaker went back to his message. So my friend didn't think there was anything significant there since the guy's name was Jeff. But then the man started to tear up. At the break they started to talk and my friend asked Jeff what that was all about. Jeff said, "Something that no one knew is that last night I was volunteering in my church's children's ministry and I was in a room of about 12 to 15 eight-year old kids and there was an eight-year old boy that was so obnoxious he was driving me nuts. He saw "Jeff" on my nametag last night and the entire time he kept saying, "I want to call you Jeffery. Can I call you Jeffery? I want to call you Jeffery. Can I call you Jeffery?" And that went on until I couldn't take it any longer and I got down on one knee, took him by the shoulders and said to him, "Look, I only let people that love me very, very much call me Jeffery." And 24 hours later a man in the middle of a lecture stops in his tracks, points to Jeff, and says, "God wants to call you Jeffery."

That was quite a powerful moment! Again, information changes the way we think, but revelation changes the way we believe.

Living a life of freedom isn't about trying harder, but it's about hearing the voice of God.

Chapter 11

How Do We Know When It's God Speaking?

Whenever I am asked this question, "How do I know if it's God speaking to me?" I always encourage people to use what I term, "The Three Harbor Lights" to confirm God's voice. Back in the 15th and 16th centuries, long before there was GPS, sailors had to depend on the stars for navigation. One of the most dangerous parts of the voyage wasn't the open seas, but entering an unfamiliar port. Underwater reefs, sandbars, and rocks threatened to sink any ship that strayed off course in the least. To help guide these ships safely into the harbor, a three light system was developed.

The first light was placed at the back of the harbor. The second light was placed at the entrance. When the approaching captain saw the light at the entrance of the harbor, he ordered a third light, a lantern, to be hung at the bow of the ship. From the captain's wheel, he would then alter his course so that the bow of the ship was in perfect alignment with the other two lights, allowing him to see just one light. If the lights weren't lined up, he knew he was off course. Today we have three similar lights that will lead us safely into the harbor of God's will for our lives.

The First Harbor Light (Located at the back of the harbor on the solid rock) **- God's Word**

The first Harbor Light is God's Word, the Bible. When God speaks to us it will always line up with the Word of God. It will never contradict God's Word. Nothing is more powerful than a Rhema word spoken personally to our situation. However, a Rhema word must be based on the Logos or written Word of God.

If I gave you directions and told you at the end of the driveway you need to turn right; but then I wrote down directions that indicated at the end of the drive go east, I would be saying the same thing (assuming turning right will take in an easterly direction). Both sets of instructions are in perfect harmony, they are just said with different words. In the same way, whenever God speaks revelation to you it will always match His written Word.

The Second Harbor Light (Located at the entrance, guiding us in) - **Peace of God**

The second Harbor Light is the peace of God that bears witness to what we believe God is saying to us. When God speaks to us it will produce the fruit of the Spirit. Galatians 5:22-23 (NKJV) describes the fruit of the Spirit as, "love, joy, peace, longsuffering, kindness, goodness, faithfulness, gentleness, self-control." When God speaks a word of revelation to our hearts, He will confirm it with the fruit of the Spirit; often with peace.

If God calls you to do something incredibly challenging, you will know if it's God because His challenge to you will be accompanied by His peace. Even if the circumstances are challenging, He will give you peace in the midst of the challenge.

The Third Harbor Light (located at the bow of the ship) - Spiritual Oversight

When God speaks to you, it will be confirmed by those who have spiritual oversight over you. This is often your pastor, although it can also be another person of solid spiritual maturity whom you trust. When God speaks to you and you bring the message to your spiritual oversight person, it is important to be open to their direction. If God does not confirm that word through them, you should consider it to not be lining up with the other Harbor Lights. This should cause you to pause and reconsider the word you received.

Many times I have people coming to tell me, "God wants me to (fill in the blank with a crazy idea)." They never ask for my opinion or thought, so I rarely give it, knowing that hidden reefs await the shipwreck.

Even pastors need to have all three harbor lights, including this third light. I have several people on my staff whom I trust in this capacity. If I make a mistake and act on something that isn't God, it not only affects me but it also affects other families. I am a firm believer pastors need to have other pastors and elders to give oversight to their lives.

The three Harbor Lights should be used for all the major decisions in life: Who to marry, where to live, what to do, when to build, etc. This system has proven itself over and over again to lead people safely into the "harbor" or to avoid a "hidden reef."

There will be times we hear from God, but it's not the right season. This is a very important point to understand. Your oversight pastor might say something like, "I think that's God, but I think it's instruction to 'prepare' for it, not to actually do it at this moment." It's very important to have this type of discernment from trusted oversight.

When God Speaks We Must Act in Agreement

We have established that God desires to give you a "Rhema" word that will transform and empower your life. When God speaks that Rhema word to you, and after you confirm that word with the Three Harbor Lights, you must then confess that word.

Romans 10:8-9 (NKJV) says, "But what does it say? 'The word (Rhema) is near you, in your mouth and in your heart' (that is, the word of faith that we preach); that if you confess with your mouth the Lord Jesus and believe in your heart that God has raised Him from the dead, you will be saved." The Greek word for confess is "homologos." This word is derived from "homo" meaning "same" and "logos" meaning "conversation, spoken word, God's Word."

So this is what He is saying, "My 'Rhema' word is in your mouth and in your heart" or "I have put My word on the tip of your tongue." Have you ever recalled a very meaningful scripture? He is saying, "I have put My word on the tip of your tongue." Then it goes on, "If you will 'homologos'" (if you will say what I just spoke to you) amazing things will happen. If you will say or confess what I just put in your heart (that Jesus is Lord and believe in your heart that God raised him from the dead), then you will be saved - a miracle happens! The natural connects with the supernatural.

I firmly believe why many Christians get frustrated that their prayers aren't answered is that they are not taking the time to hear what God is trying to say so they can simply repeat what He is saying. Jesus instructed us in Matthew 6:10 (NIV) to "Pray this way...Your will be done."

For there to be power and energy, there has to be a circuit that is connected and if you break that circuit there is no power. But when you complete the circuit there is light, power and energy that flows through. God speaks to us and we are simply to repeat back to Him what He puts on our hearts. When we confess that (homologos – say what He is saying), and say that out loud in faith, it connects and supernatural things result.

So What happens if I'm not saying what God is saying? What happens if I just decide I want a Cadillac and I start confessing a Cadillac? Are those His words? Is that homologos? Is that matching what He is saying? No, that's matching what "I" am saying. I have to listen to what **"He" is saying**.

This changes our prayer time from going into our prayer closet with a list of demands and wants to, instead, waiting upon the Lord and listening to what He is speaking to us, then simply repeating it out loud.

In Ezekiel 37:1-7, God takes the prophet Ezekiel out to a valley of dead dry bones and the Lord said, "Declare to these bones life and I will bring them together." He said, "Prophesy over these bones and I will bring these bodies back to life." In verse 7 it says, "So I prophesied as I was commanded." He did as he was told. God gave him the words and he repeated the words. He said, "Let there be life" and the dry bones literally came together and formed muscle and tissue and came to life.

Did Ezekiel do it? No. He didn't even have the thought to do it. God spoke it and commanded Ezekiel to say the same. When Ezekiel repeated (homologos) what God was saying, there was a connection between the natural and the supernatural.

In the first chapter of Luke the angel, Gabriel, visited Mary and told her she would be with child. Mary could have said, "That's impossible. I'm a virgin. It just can't happen." Instead she said, "Tell me how this will happen." The angel said, "The Spirit of the Lord will cover you and you will conceive and He will be the Son of God." Then Mary repeated back, "As your servant, let it be done as you say." She simply repeats back what God has already spoken.

Several years ago there was a gentleman by the name of Tim who attended our church. He was an executive at a local company in the area. As he walked in the door on Sunday morning he heard the Holy Spirit say to him, "Tim, if they offer prayer time during the service, if you go up front I will heal you." Tim had diabetes and was taking insulin shots multiple times a day. He thought that was weird and that those were simply his own thoughts and not God because he had never seen the service stopped to offer prayer for healing.

Meanwhile, with no awareness what God was saying to Tim, I was worshipping in the front row and during the second song I felt God saying, "If you will stop the singing and offer prayer, I will do amazing things." I stood there thinking that it was just me thinking those thoughts and not God. I began getting real nervous and entered into an "argument" in my head about whether or not it was God speaking to me: "It is God; no, it's not; yes, it is; no, it's not." Then I began wondering what if it was just me and I stopped the singing, asked people to come forward for prayer only to find that no one comes forward? If it's not God I was concerned that I would look pretty stupid. I thought, "Okay, I'm not doing that." Then I thought, "But what if it is God and I refuse to do it. Do I think He's going to ask me again to do something like that?"

After battling this in my mind, I finally determined I would rather do it and be wrong than to just refuse to do what I believed God was telling me to do just because it may make me look foolish. So I walked up on the stage and the worship leader didn't know what was going on. I just said to the congregation, "We're going to bring the music down and if you need prayer, God wants to do something amazing." Tim was sitting in the second to the last row right on the aisle and he came right up to the front for prayer. I prayed for him but

135

there were no lightning bolts or angels singing. I also prayed for a few other people. I didn't know God had already spoken to Tim. But Tim called the next day and said, "I'm going to see my doctor because since you prayed I have not taken an insulin shot." He went to his doctor and went back for follow-up visits. He has all the medical documentation showing he was a diabetic and now does not require any insulin. That was over six years ago! He was completely healed! Did I start a new ministry and ask to be invited to other cities because I can now heal diabetes? No. God spoke and put His words on my tongue for that moment and I simply repeated those words back to the congregation. In that moment my natural touched His supernatural and a miracle occurred.

Will you take time to listen to what God is saying? Jesus tells us in Matthew 6:31-33 (NKJV), "Therefore do not worry, saying, 'What shall we eat?' or 'What shall we drink?' or 'What shall we wear?' [32] For after all these things the Gentiles seek. For your heavenly Father knows that you need all these things. But seek first the kingdom of God and His righteousness, and all these things shall be added to you." Jesus instructs us not to worry, but to seek the Kingdom of God and His righteousness.

When we seek His kingdom first, He will even give us the words to speak. **Don't read the Word of God simply to read, read to listen**. He will give us the prayer we should be praying. When we are saying the same thing, then our natural will connect with His supernatural and amazing things will happen.

Understanding the principles of the Kingdom of God and living out those principles will have a life-transforming effect on our lives.

Chapter 12

Living in the Kingdom

Living in the Kingdom of God is synonymous with living in a supernatural realm. So, exactly how are we supposed to do that? How do we experience the power of God? How do we live in the natural, but connect with the supernatural?

Let's look at these questions in light of what Jesus said in Matthew 4:17. The entire ministry of Jesus was based on teaching principles related to "the Kingdom of Heaven." Jesus began to preach the good news (gospel) of the Kingdom of Heaven when he said, "Repent, for the Kingdom of Heaven is at hand" (Matthew 4:17 NKJV). This was just the first of many, many references He would make to the Kingdom of Heaven or the Kingdom of God. These two terms are used interchangeably in the New Testament.

In this passage Jesus wasn't saying, "You better straighten up because Dad's coming home and he's going to be mad." Rather, He was calling us to *true* repentance. I have discovered over many years of ministry that repentance is a misunderstood subject. To repent doesn't simply mean "to change direction." No, it's actually much more than that. To repent means to *change the way you think*. We are called to change the way we think and begin thinking like God thinks. Why? Because the "Kingdom of God is at hand." If we are to participate in the "Kingdom of God," we must repent or think differently.

In Genesis, Adam and Eve had the privilege of eating fruit from the Tree of Life. While they enjoyed this source provided to them by the eternal God, their natural life interacted with the supernatural power of God. They didn't know any other way to live except in relationship to the supernatural.

However, when Adam and Eve sinned by eating the fruit from the Tree of the Knowledge of Good and Evil they were cut off and were no longer allowed to eat of the Tree of Life. They were separated from God and the source of life.

In Matthew 7, Jesus comes and proclaims that things have changed and once again the Kingdom of Heaven is back within our grasp. We are once again invited to partake of the life-giving source that is provided by our Heavenly Father and the requirement for participation is to change how we think or "repent." Understanding the principles of the Kingdom of God and living out those principles will have a life-transforming effect on our lives.

The Kingdom Of God is Like a Budget App for a Smart Phone

If you have a smart phone you are probably familiar with the many apps that are available to you. A few years ago I decided it would be helpful to keep my budget on an app on my phone. I probably downloaded a half dozen budget apps at different times to try them out. I would put in all the pertinent numbers for our budget. My wife would call me and ask how much we had available to spend on groceries. I would look at the app and then text her back saying this is how much we have budgeted for groceries. Or she would be somewhere and find this great deal on shoes and ask me how much we had left in the clothing budget and I would check and text her back.

This seemed to work okay until I came across an app that changed everything. It had the ability to "sync." That meant I could punch in the numbers for our budget into my phone and it would automatically update my tablet. And, my wife, on the other side of town, could look at the same app on her phone and see what I just added. It was amazing! It was all in "sync!" So I could literally be looking at this app while she is finding this great deal on a pair of shoes (and any woman knows any deal on shoes is a good deal) and right before my eyes, as she pays for them and enters that information into the app, I can see that line item in the budget go down to fifty cents (just kidding). But the point is that *everything "syncs."*

In similar fashion, we can go through life somewhat independent of the supernatural, but when we learn to "sync" our lives with the Kingdom of God and the power of God, it then becomes very powerful. We no longer come to God just to unload our problems and concerns, but instead we're in "sync" with Him. We are literally on the same page. Then God can work in us and through us to accomplish His will.

Understanding the Gospel

What is the Gospel? Most people would say, "It's the good news that Jesus came to earth, died for our sins and rose again so we can have eternal life." That is 100% true. In fact, that truth is foundational to who we are and what we believe. However, that is only a portion of the gospel – the gospel of redemption.

But there's more to the gospel. Matthew 4:23 (NKJV) tells us, "And Jesus went about all Galilee, teaching in their synagogues, preaching the gospel of the kingdom." Jesus preached the "gospel" or "good news" from the very beginning of his ministry before his death and resurrection. He couldn't talk about the cross and the resurrection in past tense because it had not yet happened. Yet, it did not hamper the effectiveness of his ministry in any way and it did not hinder him from preaching the gospel.

So the gospel is not just about the death, burial and resurrection of Jesus. It is also about the good news of the Kingdom of Heaven. Much of Jesus's teaching was focused on parables which helped paint a picture of the principles of the Kingdom of Heaven. Thirteen times in the book of Matthew Jesus said, "The Kingdom of Heaven is like…." He would then tell a story that the people of that day could understand and relate to which would give them insight into what this "Kingdom" He was always talking about. At the end of each parable he would say, "Let those who have ears, hear" or "Let those who have eyes, see."

Even when Jesus taught the disciples to pray He incorporated the Kingdom. In Matthew 6:9-10 (NIV) he instructed the disciples in this manner, "This, then, is how you should pray: …Your kingdom come, Your will be done on earth as it is in heaven." Jesus was syncing two worlds together in that moment – heaven and earth. It is God's desire to sync us to the supernatural nature of His Kingdom. In fact, if we don't embrace the totality of the Kingdom of Heaven, we can fall victim to a life that is described in 2 Timothy 3:5 (NIV): "…having a form of godliness but denying its power."

Connecting with God can be somewhat scary because it means we have to give up control. It means we have to trust in some things that we can't quite figure out and that we don't understand. But when we do sync with God and His Kingdom principles, His power will begin to move in our lives in amazing ways.

Let's review the Tree of Life and the Tree of the Knowledge of Good and Evil from Genesis 2 as a reference point for the Kingdom Jesus is proclaiming. In the garden there is a tree with "life" hanging on it. God named it The Tree of Life. In that same garden there also was a tree God named The Tree of the Knowledge of Good and Evil and he gave very specific instructions to Adam and Eve to not eat the fruit from that tree. Obviously, the fruit must have looked like it could be tasty and satisfying. Yet, Adam and Eve were under very strict orders concerning that tree.

In the garden Adam and Eve had perfect communion with God. They had the ability to see the supernatural as real as the

143

natural. There was no distinction. They could see the supernatural life that God created just as you see objects in this room. They were blessed with this incredible ability to see both the natural and the supernatural. It was just the way of life God had created for them to enjoy. The fruit on The Tree of Life was not an apple, but it was a supernatural fruit that could be seen with the human eye by Adam and Eve. Why was that? Because at that time, the Kingdom of God was on earth as it was in heaven. They were in "sync" with their creator.

However, when Adam and Eve sinned, they "unplugged" from the "Tree of Life." They instead tried to get their source and their substance from the "Tree of the Knowledge of Good and Evil." When they did this, all of a sudden they had to figure out something that they never had to figure out before and that was, "What is going to be my substance of life?"

For the first time Adam and Eve had to figure out life based on their knowledge rather than the power of God. They now had to figure out their problems based on their own knowledge and the best thing they could come up with was, "We better cover ourselves." Their first action was to begin to hide themselves from God. Genesis 3:22 (NIV) records, "And the Lord God said, 'The man has now become like one of us, knowing good and evil. He must not be allowed to reach out his hand and take also from the Tree of Life and eat, and live forever.'"

Notice the wording; "He must not be allowed to reach out his hand and take also from the fruit of the Tree of Life" anymore.

He is now cut off from the Tree of Life. Mankind was not longer connected to or in sync with the supernatural.

But there is GOOD NEWS! In the New Testament we see the gospel of the Kingdom of God being preached because Jesus is trying to restore the world where the supernatural and the natural come together. Man was no longer to reach out with his hand and take from the Tree of Life. We lost our connection to our source of life – God. But Jesus came to restore that connection.

Look at what 1 Corinthians 15:45 (NIV) says about this, "So it is written: 'The first man Adam became a living being'; the last Adam, a life-giving spirit." So Jesus came to restore our connection to the Tree of Life just as Adam enjoyed. Jesus is the last Adam. He has come to restore what the original Adam lost. That is why Jesus came preaching the good news of the Kingdom of Heaven because living in the Kingdom of Heaven enables us to connect to the supernatural.

From Matthew 4:17 and forward, Jesus's message was "Repent, for the Kingdom of Heaven is at hand." As was previously mentioned, to repent is to change the way we think. By changing the way we think we will also change our beliefs. By changing our beliefs we will also change our behavior.

Jesus is introducing a paradigm shift to His audience. He was telling them (and us) we must change the way we think because the Kingdom of Heaven is right here. When Jesus said the "Kingdom of Heaven is at hand," He wasn't referring to time.

He was referring to location – "Reach out and take hold of the Kingdom." It's "at hand" or "within your reach."

I grew up believing God was way up there in the heavens, very far away, and you had to go through a bunch of intercessors for him to even hear your prayers. But Jesus is saying there are no curtains or need of sacrifices you must make to get to God because the Kingdom of Heaven is here in such a way that if you reach out you can touch it.

Our mission is to change the way we think and understand we can now grab hold of and touch the power of God in our life; it's within an arm's reach. We are no longer a citizen of this world, but we are citizens of the Kingdom of Heaven and we should live accordingly. Yes, we are still in this earthly world, but we are not part of this world. We don't wrestle against flesh and blood and the things of the natural world, but we wrestle against powers and principalities. Jesus came to assure us that we can be connected again to our Creator and to tell us that all power and authority in the Kingdom of God is right here in our hands.

How do we connect with the power of the Kingdom of Heaven?

In the Book of John there is an account recorded of a Samaritan woman at a well and Jesus met her there to tell her how to "sync" her broken natural life with the supernatural power of God. It was a cultural taboo for a man to be talking to a woman, much less a Jew to be talking to a Samaritan woman.

In John 4:13-14 (NKJV) as the Samaritan woman is drawing water out of the well Jesus said to her, "Whoever drinks of this water will thirst again. But whoever drinks the water that I shall give him will never thirst, but the water I shall give him will become within him a fountain of water springing up into everlasting life." The woman then replied to Jesus in verse 15, "Sir, give me this water that I may not thirst nor come here to draw water again."

She was listening with her natural ears, but she wasn't understanding the spiritual message. She thought, "You mean you have water I can drink out of a cup and I won't ever have to come down, in the heat of the sun, and stand in line here every day? You've got some kind magic water? Give me this water so I don't have to come here and stand in line." She was thinking in the natural. But Jesus is trying to get her to change the way she thinks.

"The woman said, "Sir, give me this water that I may not thirst or come here to draw." And Jesus said, 'Go call your husband and come here.'" (John 4:15-16 NKJV) Notice, Jesus isn't telling the woman, "No." But he is trying to unplug her from her life source; her knowledge of good and evil. She is convinced that her fulfillment in life is only one relationship away. She believed her next relationship would fulfill everything in her life. She was divorced five times and now is living with a man who is not her husband. Her life source told her that her happiness would be found in a relationship.

When Jesus told her to go get her husband, he was trying to unplug her from her life source so he could connect her with the true life source; to the fountain of living water. He's trying to get her to make a paradigm shift. He's trying to get her to have "ears that hear" and "eyes that see."

The woman answered him and said, "I have no husband." (John 4:17 NKJV) And Jesus said to her, "You have well said, 'I have no husband,' for you have had five husbands, and the one whom you now have is not your husband, that you spoke truly." (John 17-18 NKJV) Jesus is seeing a woman trapped in her own hurts and wounds.

What makes this a powerful story is that Jesus isn't saying, "Clean up your act. Act better and maybe you can figure this thing out so it will make sense." Here is a woman who was in a sense her own worst enemy because she has created this situation in her life and he sees that she is trapped; and out of mercy and love he begins to approach her. As she begins to question and to thirst and to hunger for truth and answers to her life, he begins to reveal the power of the Kingdom of God. Jesus was offering her an answer to bring her healing and freedom.

When Jesus told her she had been married five times and the man she was now with was not her husband, the woman responded, "I perceive you are a prophet" (John 4: 19 NKJV). All of a sudden she begins to see with eyes that had not seen before and she was able to hear with ears that had not heard before. Jesus was trying to convey to her, "If you knew who I was, you would reach out your hand and touch the power of God and never thirst again," (based on John 4:14).

Jesus knew if this woman would accept the living water, she would never again be thirsty for fulfillment in your life. And He offers the same opportunity to each of us. Not only will He quench that thirst for life, but He will give you power and rivers flowing with life. Jesus is saying, "I didn't come so that you would just 'get by.' I have come to give you life and life more abundantly." The abundant life is found when our natural syncs and connects with the supernatural power of God through the restorative power of Jesus, the only mediator between God and mankind.

What does the Kingdom of Heaven look like?

The Kingdom of God is the essence of God. If the Kingdom of God is the essence of God, then what is the "essence of God?" 1 John 4:8 (NKJV) says, "God is love" (NKJV). Romans 14:17 (NKJV) says, "For the kingdom of God is…righteousness and peace and joy in the Holy Spirit." While not an exhaustive list, we can say, based on these scriptures, the basic components of the Kingdom of God are love, righteousness, peace and joy.

As we bask in the atmosphere of the Kingdom, we begin to take on the nature of the Kingdom. Peace is a tangible state of the atmosphere that if we will just breathe it in, it will change us. It will take away your anxiety and turn it into something completely different. It will take your concerns about the present and the future and smash them into the ground and overwhelm you with peace. "Peace that passes all understanding" (Philippians 4:7) isn't the result of figuring it out on our own and then feeling better. But it's the presence and power of God that comes in and overwhelms those things that were once overwhelming you.

Absorbing the Kingdom of God in our lives will make us think differently. It's not about changing the content of our minds; it's about changing the process of our minds. Where we previously looked with the eyes of our head, we now look with the eyes of our heart. Where we previously comprehended with our intellect, we now comprehend with our heart. If you think differently, you will change the way you see. If you change the way you see, you will turn around and go in a different direction.

The Kingdom of Heaven is Like an Oven

The Kingdom of Heaven is an oven or an inferno of life, power, love, joy and righteousness. It is an atmosphere filled with the presence and the reality and the nature of God.

An oven also has an "atmosphere." When you turn on the oven to 350 to 400 degrees, the atmosphere is hot. Anything you put into the oven then becomes a recipient of the atmosphere of that heat. Cookie dough doesn't decide to become a cookie. Brownie batter doesn't decide to become a brownie. The heat simply has an effect on those items when they are put in the oven.

In much the same way, the atmosphere of the Kingdom of God also has an effect on all who enter it. It has capabilities to operate under its own nature and impose its nature on anything that enters it. Our role is to, "Seek first the Kingdom of God." When we seek the Kingdom of God, turn our attention to it, enter it, and tune into the voice of God, it will have an effect upon us. We will be transformed by the atmosphere of the Kingdom.

Some will be sitting outside the Kingdom unbaked, some will be half-baked, while others will be fully baked inside God's oven of love, righteousness, peace and joy. God's desire is for you to enter into the oven of the Kingdom of God and be influenced by the atmosphere that is the essence of the eternal God and creator of all things. The Kingdom of God will do for you what is impossible for you to do for yourself. Your participation in this life-giving Kingdom will reconnect you to the Tree of Life God intended for you to partake of from the beginning. Don't stay outside the oven. Don't sit on the sidelines. Drink of the living water and you will thirst no more.

In the first chapter of this book I asked you to seriously think about the answers to these questions: How do you define freedom? What does a free person feel like and act like? What does freedom look like? How do you achieve real freedom? I also encouraged you to write your answer on the page where the questions were asked or possibly in a journal. Now, after reading this book, I would like you to again contemplate these same questions and write down your answers. Then, compare your answers to what you wrote previously. Did your answers change? Do you have a different perspective on the meaning of freedom and how to achieve real freedom?

As you apply the principles that have been shared in these pages, I pray you will experience the freedom and abundant life God desires for you. Don't allow the lies of the enemy to destroy your life or your relationships any longer. Replace all those lies with the truth of God's Word and you will embark on an amazing journey that will enable you to know what it means to be *Living Free*.

Made in the USA
Monee, IL
04 February 2020

21296436R00085